THE LANGUAGE OF WHISKY

by David McNicoll

The Language of Whisky

First paperback edition 2020

ISBN: 978-1-7335682-1-0 (paperback)

Library of Congress Control Number 2019937281

Published by Wheatfield Press, LLC
www.wheatfieldpress.com

TABLE OF CONTENTS

FOREWORD

David McNicoll's book, "*The Language of Whisky*" is just the kind of book a whisky fan needs to come along at this time. We're awash in an age of random factoids and misinformation, of marketing legends told as truths and disconnected stories with little context populated by minor characters of dubious origin. All to sell us whisky. David dares to take the long form, the in-depth look into what makes the whisky we so enjoy drinking so wonderful; why it was made, who made it, and importantly, where. And he does it without being pedantic or boring. I'd dare say that the great Michael Jackson would have given it his blessing.

It's set in Scotland with a nod to its Irish ancestry, but it's here, in Scotland, where the practice of distilling the Gael's *uisge beatha*, the water of life, became a heritage, a national obsession, and an economic driver. And it's here where "*The Language of Whisky*" takes its own unique pathway. Whisky isn't just made; it is born of the people of the glens and valleys, the waterways and the rolling hills of Scotland, each with their own history and magic steeped in antiquity. In revealing the meaning behind the names of Laphroaig, Kintyre, and the dependable Macallan, we can peer back into the thousand years prior to their births. Why were there so many Glenlivets, what is an Aberlour and how did Speyside become so popular? David's answers give us insight not only into the land and the people but the reasons and motivations to create what became great whisky.

David saves whisky production for the last chapter, a strategic move. Too often we get obsessed with process without the hindsight of its origin, turning something as gloriously rich as whisky into just another commodity. After understanding the where and the why, his revelation of the how fits comfortably into this unfolding narrative. From the difference between pot and column distillation to the coopering of barrels to the production of peat, "*The Language of Whisky*" opens up whisky production to the novice and aficionado alike, in just the same way as two drops of water opens whisky's magic in your glass.

Pour a dram and crack the spine; they'll go well together.

—Robin Robinson, Robin Robinson, LLC,
a boutique sales/marketing consultancy to the spirits industry

ACKNOWLEDGEMENTS

I was born and grew up amid the stunning scenery of the Perthshire Highlands in the heart of Scotland. I guess whisky was always in my DNA—while sadly I never got to meet him, my grandfather worked at Aberfeldy Distillery. When leaving university, I also went to work at a distillery: Blair Athol, in the town of Pitlochry, and there my love and passion for the juice was born; not only a passion for how it was made and how we taste it, but its social and cultural heritage; something that has never left me.

When I moved to the United States, I thought I'd teach the locals a thing or two—I couldn't have been more wrong. America is a country with a sophisticated palate; it was me that needed to learn a thing or two. I landed lucky. I had the opportunity to meet and be sharply educated by the legend that is Jimmy Russell down at Wild Turkey, and to learn more about Scotch in an afternoon than I did in eight years previous by my good friend Iain McCallum, master blender and former distillery manger. This has stood me in good stead as I embark on this journey. The support of friends here in New York, like Mike at the Caledonia whisky bars, and Tommy at the Flatiron Room, among a myriad of others, have made this book possible. I'd like to give special mention to Robin Robinson, a true guru in the whisky world, for providing the foreword for this endeavor. Thank you, sir, and the next dram's on me.

But, most of all—we talk about a labor of love, but we don't truly realize it's the love of others that makes that true. My amazing wife, Erin; my beautiful twins, Alasadair and Cameron; and of course, back home in Scotland, my parents, Alan and Christine, and the regulars at the bars in the beautiful Cathedral City of Dunkeld. That support just makes a dream come true, and I cannot thank you enough.

A book isn't just about sitting down at a computer and writing words. It's a recording of life's experiences and the people you meet on that journey. We Celts are an emotional, introspective, and dark race. But thank the Almighty, He gave us whisky to see us through it all!! *Slàinte mhath!*

PART 1

THE WATER OF LIFE

Malt whisky is like the Scots tongue—broadly one language yet, within that, so many different dialects, each one unique to its own distillery. It is this subtle distinction which gives every malt its unmistakable identity.

—Highland Park Brochure

Scotch whisky is a phenomenon: our national drink is sold in nearly two hundred countries from Norway to New Zealand and back again (this global reach is comparable to Coca-Cola), and accounts for a staggering one hundred eighty million Imperial Gallons of the amber nectar. There are those who enjoy a wee dram from time to time, perhaps for a special occasion or in the company of friends; others who imbibe a snifter or two before or after dinner; a nightcap even. Then there are those who are real enthusiasts, with cupboards bursting with a good range and who love to go to tastings or are always on the lookout for something new. There are people out there who collect rare and valuable whiskies, probably, and rather sadly, never to be opened investments made by spending crazy amounts of money (at the time of writing, a bottle of Macallan was recently sold for around £850,000 (approximately $1.1 million)). Whichever category you fall into, this book is for you.

This book is for you if you've ever been in a decent bar with a good range of whiskies and wondered how to pronounce half of them, what the names mean, and what the origins are of the famous and not so famous whiskies that stand guard on the back bar. This book is for you if you've ever had to sit and listen to some self-appointed whisky expert drone on about this and that in a language that seems utterly alien (don't worry, half the time it's opinionated baloney anyway). This book is for you if you are interested in whisky, Scotland, history, or all three.

There are legions of books out there on the subject of whisky, and they range from the excellent to the dire. Most of them tend to focus on production and flavor, or perhaps the heritage of a particular area. There is no need to add another taste or checklist-style book to this pantheon. Whisky is a global drink, a universal language that we all understand. So, the idea here is to peel back the layers to find out the story behind the names, all against the backdrop of Scottish history, as the two are inexorably linked. It is a chance to open the window and see the world of our forefathers, to look through their eyes. For each distillery, in its name, takes us back to a long-forgotten time when our landscape was painted in different strokes.

Whisky making and drinking seems to have its own language as well—words and terms that also have a heritage and purpose. Here, too, I'll try to sweep away the fluff and pretentiousness and guide you through the minefield: from the barley harvest to your taste buds. It's a fascinating journey—come along and enjoy the ride. We begin our story by explaining why Scotch became the global superstar it did. Grab a glass, pour your dram, and sit back.

CHAPTER 1

SCOTCH-LAND:
THE RISE OF A SUPERPOWER

The proper drinking of Scotch whisky is more than indulgence: it is a toast to civilization, a tribute to the continuity of culture, a manifesto of man's determination to use the resources of nature to refresh mind and body and enjoy to the full the senses with which he has been endowed.
—David Daiches

Most peoples and cultures around the world have at some point developed the art of fermenting beverages (the process of which will be explained in Part Three), which put simply, is how to make booze. This is a mere imitation of nature: both our own physiology and observations of monkeys getting drunk on ripening fruit indicates a sense of enjoyment, and indeed a nutritional value in consuming alcohol by us and our ancestors going back millions of years. Given the season, grapes will ferment on the vine and it's not a big jump to realize that this can be replicated, refined, and controlled.

From the drunken monkey theory to Biblical times ("and he [Noah] drank of the wine and was drunken" – Genesis 9:21), man has experimented, manipulated, and tasted every possible concoction from every conceivable organic material. Geography and climate played a huge role in the eventual evolution of the particular drink of choice in any given region; in Europe, that tended to mean wine in the Mediterranean and the mid-continent from a grape base, and in the Baltic and North Sea lands, beer from a wheat, barley, or rye base.

Two thousand years ago, the Roman Empire reached all the way to Hadrian's Wall in what is now northern England; the soldiers no doubt drank wine fermented and aged in the sun-soaked lands of Italy or France, exported all the way to very homesick legionaries stationed on the windswept Cheviot Hills. The local chiefs probably bartered and bought this exotic drink (vineyards are not viable beyond the far south of England) and felt empowered, perhaps even giddy (if you pardon the pun), and an empathy with the Pax Romana. For the most part, the locals drank crude ales and beers, as barley and bere (a less productive, but hardier strain of barley that can cope with wet climates and from where the word 'beer' comes) were just about the only crops that grew in these unforgiving climes.

Be it wine, beer, or mead, which is made from honey, the maximum level that could be achieved by fermentation was generally around 10 percent by volume, rarely more than 15 percent, and never more than 20 percent. When we consider the pantheon of high-volume spirits on the back bar of every modern pub, our forefathers were fairly limited in how they got their kicks from the brew, and they often augmented it with hallucinogens such as mushrooms and hemp. Not that everyone was drinking to oblivion, and whether it was beer, ale, or fine wine, there were occasions and events when those in higher society drank for social reasons and in moderation, as we do today. But for all that, be assured that alcohol was very much part of the fabric of the daily lives of the ordinary folk carving out a living from the land—a farming existence upon which these drinks were a welcome byproduct and a way to escape hardships and miseries that we cannot fathom in this day and age.

A climate change around two thousand years ago meant a rise in sea levels, and this, it would appear, made the waters of the lower Nile increasingly brackish; that is, saltier and thus less drinkable. These ancient Egyptians, in order to combat the environmental catastrophe facing them, began to distill these waters to remove the offending salt and make it potable. Water boils at or around 100°C (depending on altitude and pressure), and by turning it to steam and then back to water, any solids and salts will be separated. It was a knowledge that would find its way into the world of alcohol, and a knowledge that remained in the Middle East. Much of this information was collated at the famous Library at Alexandria, only to be lost to civilization when the library was periodically scorched by the Romans from the rule of Augustus to the fourth century. It's not common currency among modern scholars to refer to the "Dark Ages," but the ultimate destruction of the library, to this writer's mind, does usher in a period that may well be fitting of the term. Medieval minds would have to look to a more unlikely source to bring themselves up to speed.

At some point at the height of an Arabic period of Enlightenment around twelve hundred years ago or so, chemists discovered that alcohol boils at a lower temperature than water (around 78°C, or 172°F); which in and of itself was a hell of an understanding, considering a working thermometer wasn't invented until the seventeenth century, and concepts of scales of hot or cold were non-existent until the Polish-born Dutch citizen, Daniel Fahrenheit came up with a true sliding scale. They discovered that under certain pressures in a still (the Arabic word "alembic" is still used today to describe part of the still apparatus), vapors of ethanol, methanol, and other rarer alcohols begin to evaporate off as the heat is increased, but before the water is turned into steam. As both are clear liquids when recondensed, and without the use of modern instrumentation, these old scientists really were pushing the envelope of discovery.

The spirit these Middle Eastern pioneers were making they called, in Arabic, *al kohl*, and it's the origin of our English word "alcohol" (kohl was originally a fine powder made from stibnite in a similar way to distillation). It means "to stain or darken," for these alchemists (another Arabic derived word) weren't creating a fine drink, but were using the stuff as the base for cosmetics—eyeliner and the like. It would nomadically trek across Europe leaving footprints along the way until it reached the far-flung British Isles: the edge of the world.

Around nine hundred years ago, it was known there was a spirit being made in France and other parts of central Europe for human consumption, and of course intoxication. This would appear to have been a type of rudimentary vodka. If you keep re-distilling the spirit you will eventually end up with something that approaches 100 percent alcohol (although you can't quite get there unless you have some pretty nifty equipment). It will be colorless, odorless, and for all intents and purposes, flavorless—essentially, vodka. (Vodka comes from the Polish for "little water"—*wódka*). Don't get me wrong—there is some great vodka out there, but the flavor spectrum is less complex than whisky or brandy.

Other spirits were also being produced from around 1300 onward—some from the pulp left over from wine making (Pomace), producing, for example, Italian Grappa. Fermented fruits such as plums and pears could be distilled into a spirit mainly concentrated in places like Bavaria or Austria called "Schnapps." The root of the word is *schnappen*; a Low German word that essentially means to take back in a quick shot. Applejack, which would evolve as an American drink, is akin to schnapps but made from cider. French Calvados or Hungarian Pálinka would have a similar fruit origin.

In the Low Countries, and parts of Northern Germany, to make it more palatable, herbs and berries were added during the process, imparting flavor. Eventually, juniper berries became the herb of choice, and from the Dutch (where modern gin manufactory was pioneered) for juniper, *jenever*, we get gin. This process had its origins in southern Europe, but it was there in the Netherlands that it took form.

The original distillate of wine, which had become refined, was referred to as burnt wine (or, in German, *branntwein*) and from where we get brandy. Burnt is an old term for a distillate of alcohol rather than being set on fire.

Gin, like vodka, was generally made from low-quality grain considered unfit for beer brewing; and, another spirit, whisky, which would develop on the British Isles, has its origins from the same root. Then as now, religious houses were often the font of very good wines and spirits, from Chartreuse to Buckfast. However, monasteries in days gone by also served as makeshift hospitals (a great remnant lies upon the ancient Roman road in southern Scotland on the bleak Soutra Hill, where even today bacteriological evidence shows this was a place of healing), where the sick and lame could reach for sanctuary. As a cure-all, the monks, drawing upon knowledge gleaned from their brothers across a sort of medieval World Wide Web reaching back to the alchemists of the Middle East, distilled a concoction they called *aqua vitae*—Latin for the "Water of Life." It didn't matter what was wrong with you—this was what you were getting. Sore head? *Aqua vitae.* Broken leg? *Aqua vitae.* The Black Death? *Aqua vitae.* The knowledge was passed around the various monastic communities via a special book called the Mappae Clavicula: the "Little Key of the World," a sort of medieval Wikipedia.

Alcohol does have some medicinal qualities: to a point— it's clearly not going to cure you of the bubonic plague or leprosy. However, in a generally war-torn, famine struck, horror show of a world, where the Four Horsemen were galloping around the corner, any potential remedy was seized upon. The misery of medieval Europe would ultimately give rise to some of the greatest spirits ever made.

The Black Death came to Scotland in 1351 and killed around half of the population; and regardless of the obvious personal tragedy it brought to individuals and families, it was a social game changer. Put bluntly, Scotland's population would not recover for nearly four hundred years, as it was ravaged again and again by this horrendous plague; all against a never-ending backdrop of smallpox, typhoid, measles, and a whole host of other grim diseases that brought short lives to an even shorter end. Even in 1700, the life expectancy of someone from Edinburgh was thirty-five years if it was a day.

Aqua vitae, if something of a cliché today when we look at it, did take people away from this horror, if just for a night. And it wasn't long before people started making spirits for themselves at home and on their farms. There was a lot of space: in 1400, the population of Scotland was around 500,000—one tenth of what it is today. Not speaking Latin, they called their magic juice *uisge beatha*, a direct translation into Scots Gaelic and meaning again "water of life." This was no refined, well-matured single malt; it was an unaged barley-based moonshine. Harsh, fiery, and potent, it was a clear liquid that went from rudimentary still to lips as soon as it cooled. If you were lucky, most of it would be the drinkable alcohol: ethanol.

The arrival of high-proof spirits was a game changer for the poor farm folk of Scotland. There was also another variable in the equation. Until the 1270s, Northern Europe experienced a relative warm period—the "Age of Ale and Bread" as it was known in Scotland, where winters were milder, summers dryer, and famine and crop failure less frequent. In a way, it was the golden age before the storm of pestilence and the climatic shift to the Little Ice Age that would follow.

The Wars of Independence against the ambitions of the English king, Edward I (plus an insidious civil war of sorts between rival families claiming the right to the throne of Scotland, and the Church throwing its hat into the ring), had devastated particularly Lowland Scotland. Even after the famous victory at the Battle of Bannockburn in 1314, there was always the threat of English invasion; and then came the plague. The climate and weather fell off the cliff too, which meant more crop failure and less arable land available. All this changed society and the socio-economic structure (the clan system in the Highlands developed around this period as a way for warlords to maintain order and power amid chaos).

The Feudal system in Scotland, begun by King David I in the twelfth century, really marched apace following Bannockburn and the rise of the Bruce and Stewart dynasties. This meant organized and regulated markets, and market towns known as "Burghs." *Uisge beatha*, a by-product of the monastic and agricultural world, would soon become a commodity to be sold for those increasingly rainy days.

The first mention of whisky in Scotland comes from 1494, when Friar Jon Cor petitions the king for more malt (malted barley) to make *aqua vitae*; and recently academics at Aberdeen University have unearthed a manuscript referencing a whisky still back in 1505.

Since the Neolithic, barley has been the staple crop in Scotland; one of the few grains that can thrive in the cold wet climate of the north (the years 1400 to 1850 were especially cold and wet—sometimes summer never happened at all). In some places the soil was rich, especially in the east from Edinburgh, north to Aberdeenshire; but for most of the Highlands and Islands it was thin, acidic, and unproductive. Barely was the only option. These were subsistence farmers, no government handouts there, and they harvested grain to give to the miller to make bread, some for animal feed, some for grain seed for the next year, and the rest to make beer or a spirit. In a wet climate like Scotland, any excess grain would soon rot, so it made perfect sense to make *uisge beatha*—it could be exchanged and maybe even used to pay rent. Tough times for sure, but from there grew the greatest spirit industry of them all.

Certainly by 1600, spirit production in Scotland was all but ubiquitous north to south, east to west. Every farmer, merchant, and tinker had their small pot stills and brewed their water of life. The mercurial Highland prophet, Coinneach MacCoinneach, known as the Brahan Seer, predicted that there would be a dram shop at the head of every ploughed rig (a dram is a whisky pour of unspecified volume), and even in his own time, somewhere around four hundred years ago, he wouldn't have been far off the mark.

Starting in earnest around that time, official record keeping became normal practice at a state, town, and local government level in all of Lowland Scotland, where administration was coalescing around Edinburgh, as well as on the large country estates; and they were written in English—the language of commerce. Even in the Highlands, where the ancient Gaelic tongue was dominant, officialdom preferred to use English. So, in keeping account of what a farm, for instance, was producing for the purposes of rent and profitability, *uisge beatha* was firstly written in English as ooshky bayha (or a phonetic to this end), then ooshky, and ultimately, whisky (or whiskey in Ireland, where similar developments were taking place, but a different spelling employed).

Storm clouds were gathering though, and the story and fortune of whisky and of Scotland became inexorably linked.

∽

It began with the best of intentions: a new dawn ushering in a period of peace, stability, and prosperity. But the seventeenth century would bring a whole new raft of strife and torment for the British Isles—and change them forever.

In March 1603, King James VI of Scotland inherited the throne of England following the death of his cousin, the aged Elizabeth I. He'd been king of Scotland for thirty-six years, so was by no means wet behind the ears when he flitted from Edinburgh, went south to London, and was crowned James I of England. It was his mission in life, his obsession really, to unify his two realms (which also included Wales and Ireland) into one, which he called Great Britain. He was instrumental in getting some of this to happen, but the intransigency of both the Scots and the English to actual union hampered his ambitions. Religious unrest was always looming in the background along with political agitation amongst those great lords, landowners, and wealthy merchants in England who wanted a greater say in running the country. James, crafty and astute, was able to ride the storm; his irascible, naïve, and arrogant son, Charles I was not.

In the 1640s, The Wars of the Three Kingdoms (once called the English Civil War by historians—but today widely recognized as a conflict that tore at the heart of every part of

Britain and Ireland) pitted Parliament against King, Church against Crown, and brother against brother. What had started as a dispute over a prayer book in St Giles' Cathedral in Edinburgh would explode in every direction.

Parliament defeated the king in England and the quasi-religious Covenant movement governed in Scotland; but still the war went on. Eventually, as tends to happen in these circumstances, a strong man rises to become a dictator, ending the conflict but imposing his own will on the people. That man was, of course: Oliver Cromwell. After chopping the king's head off, dissolving Parliament, defeating the Scots, and imposing martial law, Cromwell brought stability (albeit by fear and force) to the country. Following his death in 1658 and the restoration of Charles II, England entered a period of great stability, and this led to advances in agriculture and land use. A farming revolution followed, and England's wealth and population grew exponentially. Scotland's experience was slightly different.

The fall out from the Civil War would affect the country for decades; the deep-seated animosity between the Clan Campbell-led Covenanters and the Royalists smoldered, and religious fault lines cracked. Scotland was also a war-like nation, especially in the Highlands where resources were scarce; and as a poor country, it was hard to drag itself out of the mire. The 1670s were known as "The Killing Times," as vendettas and old scores were settled. The Civil War rumbled on in all but name, and much of it sanctioned by a king who wanted to break the power of the nobles and the Church in the north. Not until the 1690s did Scotland begin to emerge from the mire that had dogged the country and its beleaguered people in the century following the Union of Crowns and James's great vision of prosperity. But sometimes the Scots can be their own worst enemy, and sometimes the dice just fall badly—we are a people dealt the wildest of cards; and the Darien fiasco would change our destiny forever.

The Scottish government, wealthy merchants, and the high aristocracy were scratching their heads as to how to bridge the yawning gap that had grown between Scotland and England. Paranoid or not, always at the back of their minds, a rich England was a constant threat. They saw that the English, now settled and politically at peace at home, had extended their reach across the seas building successful colonies in America, the Caribbean, and even in far off India. By the end of the seventeenth century, these colonies, especially in the West Indies, were generating vast amounts of profit for the English treasury. It was a truly enviable position, where wealth begat wealth. The movers and shakers in Scotland decided the country needed to go off on an imperial adventure of its own.

Probably the most famous Scot of the time was William Patterson, the man who had founded the Bank of England and championed the cause of the central lending bank (a revolutionary idea which would help England win her war against Holland, the most powerful mercantile entity at the time). So, the Scottish government turned to this mercurial genius to spearhead this colonial program. I'm not sure what due diligence Patterson did, but his choice of the Darien peninsula in Panama would prove to be a disaster. It was as if he threw a dart at a map of the world and hoped for the best.

The proposition put before the great and good of the Scottish nobility and merchant classes looked so appealing and a sure thing, that they signed up in droves—with both gold and manpower. It is reckoned that nearly a third of Scotland's movable wealth and the flower of her aristocratic youth sailed across the Atlantic to the Promised Land. Darien, however, was not Chesapeake Bay or Boston Harbor; it was a mosquito-infested, disease-ridden swamp. Worse still, it theoretically 'belonged' to Spain. It was an unmitigated, catastrophic failure. Of the four thousand or so that crossed the ocean, fewer than one hundred survived to limp into New York harbor after less than two years of fighting malaria, yellow fever, and the Spanish. And, of course, all the gold was gone. Scotland teetered on the brink of bankruptcy, with her economy in tatters and the nation facing ruin.

Hobbling into the eighteenth century and licking her wounds, the next emergency was simply waiting around the corner. There was a royal succession crisis, which led to a cold war between Scotland and England; and with Scotland in financial ruins, it was in no position to resist the demands coming from London. At length, it led to the Treaty of Union, which in 1707 resulted in the formation of a United Kingdom of Great Britain. To sweeten the medicine, the Westminster mandarins softened the treaty by allowing Scotland the right to retain her own legal system and passed other key measures that kept many of Scotland's independent customs and rights in place. Among them was Article 13, which would have a direct impact on the story of Scotch: "*That during the continuance of the Duty payable in England on Malt, which determines 24th June 1707, Scotland shall not be charged with that Duty.*" At this point, it's worth noting that malted barley is grain that has gone through a process and prepared for consumption, brewing, and whisky making (see Part Three).

Essentially, Scottish producers would be exempted from the high malt taxes incurred in England. This made a lot of sense—virtually all whisky produced in Scotland was homemade and a mainstay of life in the countryside, from personal consumption to cash-in-kind payments. Yes, some was being made commercially and sold to small markets in the growing towns of the Central Belt, but even this was small-scale, and an important cog in an economy bereft of money.

So, when Prime Minister Robert Walpole overturned Article 13 in 1724 and introduced a uniform (and thus higher for Scotland) tax rate across the United Kingdom, there was an outcry. There were riots in the streets of Edinburgh and Glasgow, and general civil disorder nationwide. So fierce was the backlash that it threatened the very union itself. Troops had to be brought in, and draconian measures introduced; and all this against the backdrop of the Jacobite cause, which looked to overthrow the current royal dynasty and replace it with the exiled Stuart family. This was not welcome by all: these were hard and uncertain times. The country was a tinderbox; and the doomed Jacobite rebellion of 1745/46 would be in some respects a manifestation of this. Its outcome would change the nation forever.

If there is one rule that holds true across the world, when taxes are raised, or prohibitions introduced on vice commodities like drugs and alcohol, it drives it underground into the realm of the black market; and this is what happened to Scotch. In addition, with the collapse of the Jacobite rebellion at Culloden Battlefield in 1746, many Highland chiefs, who'd supported the cause, fled to France. Back home, their loyal clansmen raised monies (beyond the rents and taxes the government was levying) and sent it overseas. The sale of whisky helped to raise those funds. To a London establishment that had stared down the barrel of oblivion, this was viewed as an act of treason. It was a heady mix to be sure.

The eighteenth century was the heyday of the smuggler, the illicit still and midnight shipments through the mountains. It was a game of cat and mouse, and one where the mouse invariably remained one step ahead. The government wanted to tax the whisky being produced whether by farmers in their rustic cottages or by the more commercially driven enterprises (which were generally run by merchants or cooperatives in the larger towns. We tend to think of whisky making as a rural industry, but three hundred years ago, much of it was made in towns and cities). Thus, to stamp out the smuggling and illegal production of whisky, it employed Excisemen or Gaugers (from the gauges they carried to test the spirit)—essentially a combination of tax collector and police enforcer (and at its height they were confiscating ten thousand stills a year—makes you wonder what slipped through their net).

They were hated individuals, mocked and ridiculed, and the ingenuity of the producers tested time and again their ruthless pursuits. These were the days of hide and seek, when farmers hid stills in caves and ruined cottages; an age that would come to symbolize the early romantic nature of whisky, when the people stood up against the state to protect their precious dram. It's the classic tale of "them and us" against a backdrop of majestic scenery and stories of daring-do. Robert Burns, the famous Scottish poet who wrote "Auld Lang Syne," penned a song where the Devil dances off with the exciseman, Pied Piper-style, leaving the townsfolk in peace to 'brew their malt'. Burns, a whisky-drinking lothario himself, had to take on a job as a Guager just to earn enough to feed his large brood, but his song shows how ironic he saw his position.

In the centuries to come, marketing gurus and ad-men would draw back to this time when whisky was in its infancy and being made by hardworking men and women in secret against the machinations of a state that would take the very pleasure away from the poor country folks. This "stick it to the man" attitude would prove a powerful image, and it remains with us to this day.

Scotland has long been owned by her aristocracy. Even today, vast tracts of the country still belong to various dukes, earls, and lords. These were powerful and influential men who ruled their great estates like kings. The majority of the country folk were their tenants or employees—and at best, these farmers lived a subsistence lifestyle, harsh and unforgiving. This was the way it had always been, yet a paradigm shift in social structure and economics was about to strike the land of Adam Smith, the father of capitalism. The Enlightenment would grow in the streets of Edinburgh's New Town, industry would flourish in Glasgow, Dundee, and Falkirk, and somewhat more darkly, the Highland Clearances would alter the north forever. These changes and the new order would have profound effects on both the people and the whisky that was being produced—good and bad. As whisky became a covert operation, potential markets were expanding rapidly, both in Scotland and south, in the growing big English cities, too. Whisky had by one way or another become a truly commercial industry. The tax laws would and could not last forever—the tide was turning.

By 1800, most of the whisky being made in Scotland was still being produced in secret by farmers for local or personal consumption, although there were sizeable clandestine operations in most of the principal expanding urban centers, mirroring the gin craze in London to some extent. However, some bigger players were emerging that could front the duty payable and invest openly in new techniques that would ultimately improve the quality of the product on offer. Some well known names emerge at this time—Bowmore, Oban, and Highland Park, for example—catering for a larger market and established as purely profit-making enterprises.

Figure 1.1 Strath Isla Distillery

That's not to say that some of the whiskies being made under the radar weren't of a good quality, but without an ability to invest or promote, these distillers stood at a distinct disadvantage if they wanted to operate commercially. Thus, for the most part, whisky remained as it had since the Middle Ages: a homebrew. That said, this was a two-way street. Locals with the right connections could buy illegal whisky from known sources with a nod and a wink; and commercially, this set the legal producers at a disadvantage. There was a two-fold consequence: a push for quality, and a necessity to sell to markets beyond their own backyard.

Two hundred years ago, large tracts of land around the River Spey in the eastern Highlands, whose hills were famous for good whisky, belonged to Alexander Gordon, the fourth Duke of Gordon, one of Britain's largest private landowners. Like many Highland lords, he spent much of his time in London at Court, where he hob-nobbed with the great and the good of the British aristocracy. Despite the fact his estates ran into the hundreds of thousands of acres, his income was relatively meager in comparison to those of the landed gentry in the Home Counties (the rural lands around metropolitan London), which no doubt irked His Grace, who was known to contemporaries as the "Cock of the North."

Down south, rents were paid in cash, making the landlord rich; but in the Highlands, rents were often paid in kind: rabbit skins, cheeses, eggs, and illicit whisky. It was all these poor folks could give, but it hardly made the duke a rich man. The whisky, however, was something that might. If only this myriad of whisky makers could sell their wares for cash, then maybe His Grace could be paid in cash. The duke was in a position of influence in the government and was able to convince Parliament to change the tax laws concerning malt; and in 1823 the Excise Act was passed. This removed the unpopular taxes, and for a one-off fee of £10, distillers could operate legally. This was the foundation stone of the modern Scotch whisky industry.

Overnight, hundreds of legal distilleries emerged; most of which were by nature small and farm based, although several large-scale operations emerged, such as Glen Livet, Jura, and Glen Grant. Grocery merchants like John Walker and the Chivas Brothers took advantage of the new regulations to buy the higher quality stuff and re-label as their own. In this the seeds were sown that would change the spirits industry forever. This was a practice long employed in Ireland—it was the merchants there that sold the whiskies rather than the distillers themselves usually.

Beyond the new industries and the laws around it, infrastructure changes were moving apace as Scotland (well, Lowland Scotland at least) moved from an agrarian world to a contemporary industrial landscape. It is no exaggeration to say that Scotland would change more over the course of a generation than it had since the days of the plague. According to the census, the population of Scotland in 1831 was 2,364,386, and by the eve of the First World War it had risen to 4,760,407—a doubling within a lifetime. That had to have consequences. That had to fundamentally change the fabric of society and the infrastructure that supported it: railways, steamships, turnpike roads, and of course, the vast expansion of Glasgow and Edinburgh. The Central Belt of Scotland transformed with such speed that the authorities, landlords, and services simply couldn't keep up—nor were they particularly sympathetic, and the worst slums in Europe were born. Not only did the quality of life suffer, so did the quality of water, and the distillers in the Central Belt would have to accommodate that.

These new transport links became a double-edged sword in a way. It meant that more remote producers, say in the Highlands and Islands, could transport their wares to the big Lowland markets; bridges such as the ones at Craigellachie and Dunkeld saw journey times scythed; better harbors on Islay and at Wick did the same. However, the other side of the coin meant that distillers in the Lowlands were, in terms of time and awareness, much closer to the taxman in Edinburgh. The pressure to switch from neutral spirit making to quality whisky making, but under closer government scrutiny, ultimately meant that distillers in the Central Belt were at a disadvantage. Not to mention that the relatively few water sources were either being used for an evergrowing industrial base, or were contaminated by it. These are important factors in why today there remains a discrepancy in the distribution of distilleries north and south of the Highland Line. Beyond that sentinel line things were evolving apace.

Many of the farm distilleries formed cooperatives, pulling together resources and skills, like good water supply, plentiful barley, advanced understanding in process, and great transport links. Slowly, the number of distilleries was riddled and sieved of the poorer quality, numbers of establishments dwindled, and the overall quality rose. In no time, most good distilleries were able to compete and perhaps even outdo their more commercial rivals. This was a baptism of fire that the industry needed to build a solid reputation. Advances were also made in the process. Nineteenth century whisky, while a long way from the toxic gut rot of earlier days, was still pretty robust, shall we say, unmatured in most cases, and oily. Changes to the shape and size of the stills and the move toward aging in oak casks revolutionized and improved dramatically the juice on offer. However, an invention in Ireland would change the landscape altogether.

In 1830, Aeneas Coffey designed a type of still known as a column, patent, or Coffey still. It is a tall, complex pipe that essentially makes high-proof spirit constantly. This is how modern vodka, gin, and some bourbons are made (although for bourbon, they lower the proof to retain the flavors. It's the high proof (190°) that kills the flavor in vodka). Using various grains, running the still continuously, and putting the spirit in oak barrels, you will create what's known as Grain Whisky (as opposed to the Malt Whisky being made in the traditional distilleries). It is high-proof, bland, and unpalatable stuff, but it is relatively cheap to produce, and there's plenty of it. The question for the merchants that had to sell to the market was what to do with it: how to utilize this new invention to maximize profits.

Mixing different whiskies together, particularly grains with malts, could be one answer; the strong flavors and rich fats in the malt could temper the fire and the lack of flavor in the grain. However, this form of mixing was not permitted by law; though, I'm sure plenty flouted this. Though other things like herbs, botanicals, and flavored waters were added; as was plenty of sugar and syrup, it was still pretty grim.

Strangely though, the market, which was used to potent gin and weak beer, was moving toward drinking blander and more mixable spirits. Thus, desire was there to create a Scotch that dovetailed with the consumers' growing demands. So, in 1860, the law was changed to allow the mixing of Grain and Malt Whisky, and the new term was "Blended Whisky."

In time, a set of giants would rise to dominate the industry, bringing together skills in marketing, innovation, and an innate ability to judge exactly what the consumer wanted for the product. Some were individuals like John Dewar and Jimmy Buchanan; while others, like Johnny Walker and Chivas, were well-established companies that continued to develop and master the art of the blender. As their success and wealth grew, their influence over the malt distilleries and producers became one where the tail began to wag the dog. Certainly, by the 1880s the vast bulk of all whisky being made was being sold to the blenders, as it remains to this day. It made sense then for those companies to start buying up the distilleries themselves to ensure supply, and a consistency in that supply. As the industry became increasingly corporate, it also became more monopolized, and the symbiotic relationship between producers, blenders, and marketing men skewed toward the big players. And the men at the helm would become known as the "whisky barons."

For the first time there was a concentrated, mercantile effort on the part of the industry to expand and dominate the drinks market; but there would be some good fortune along the way, too.

The Phylloxera bug is a tiny insect from the aphid family, and while the little green aphid loves to munch on rose bushes, the Phylloxera prefers grape vines. A native to North America, where vineyards locally had built up resistance, it hopped on board one of the many ships crossing the Atlantic as trade between the United States and Europe boomed; and upon arrival in France it went to town. For centuries, wine had been a mainstay both economically and culturally to many regions across France—a key element of the psyche of the country. French vineyards were, of course, not immune to the bug, and it tore through all the main wine growing areas, decimating the crop.

From its arrival in 1863 to the 1880s, nearly 90 percent of the French vineyards were utterly destroyed and output reduced by 75 percent; and then it moved on to other parts of the continent, including Germany and Italy. The French covet their wine; it's such a part of life on a day-to-day basis. Thus, a shortage was like a dagger to the heart. Wine is, of course, drunk in every home, but it is also vital in the brandy (in particular, the Cognac) industry. So, with a two-decade long dry up, it suffered badly. Brandy is the distillate of wine in the same way whisky or vodka is the distillate of beer.

In the second half of the nineteenth century, Cognac and other top brandies were the drink of choice of the wealthy and socialite classes, and with a drought, they started looking around for alternatives. The whisky barons, many of them already members of high society, moved in. By offering the middle and upper classes their better-quality blends, and marketing and packaging them as deluxe or "very old," they pandered to a vain audience, and it worked hook, line, and sinker. On both sides of the Atlantic, and across the evergrowing British Empire, those who could afford it turned to good quality Scotch.

The Imperial experience was not uniform or predictable: Britons in India still tended toward IPA beer, or gin and tonic (tonic water contains quinine, which counters many of the symptoms of malaria), for example. But wherever the Scots went, they took Scotland with them, and slowly, our national drink began to put down firm roots in every corner of the globe.

While those and such as those were switching to Scotch, the lower classes and the poor in society, especially in the big English cities like London, continued to drink gin. However, through the second half of the nineteenth century as polite Victorian society became increasingly puritanical, there were conscious moves to improve the living conditions for the very worst off in the inner-city slums; and this, too, would be part of a worldwide movement that would have profound implications for Scotch whisky.

In the nineteenth century, living conditions in the big cities of most industrial nations were horrific, to say the least. Tens of thousands of people were crammed cheek-by-jowl into slums, forced into backbreaking jobs for a pittance of pay, and faced the daily threat of killer diseases like cholera and typhoid.

Employers and the wealthy at large cared little for the poor and working classes upon whom their riches were built, but by the end of the Victorian era there was a slow but concerted move amongst certain interest groups and scions of society to help and generally improve the lives of those at the very bottom. It was a multi-pronged attack: housing was upgraded, clean water supplies installed, effective sewage management instigated, and working conditions advanced. But it was also recognized that the poor had to help themselves as well.

Gin, or "Mother's Ruin," was seen by the same people forcing through improvements as being the worst scourge of them all—destroying lives, inhibiting productivity, and promoting violence and criminality. Cities were full of gin dens, as they were called, where for a few pennies you could crash-out and forget the horrors of life in a temporary solace found at the bottom of a bottle.

We think of alcohol and substance abuse as a relatively modern affliction, but our great-grandparents drank far more than we do. Lord Braxfield, one of Scotland's most notorious "hanging" judges would consume at least two gallons of wine every trial. We are a sober nation in comparison to our forefathers. Still, then like today, there were moves abroad in the land to wipe alcoholism, and indeed alcohol itself, from the map; and it took on a life of its own. There was also a severe puritanical streak; from society ladies with time to spare and money to spend, to canting clergymen. Poverty was seen as being a sin in itself, and that hunger and strife were good "incentives" for people to work. It is euphemistically called the "Protestant Work Ethic." It was all wrapped up in an air of superiority spiced with a need to have the poor working hard to make the rich richer. Having them escape to the bottom of a bottle simply didn't fit with this viewpoint. So, packaged as charity and help, those ulterior motives influenced a policy imposed on a group in society that were pretty much owned and browbeaten by those selfsame people. It was a world of "Don't do as I do; do as I say."

By the late nineteenth century, there were numerous abolitionist groups (collectives lobbying for the prohibition of alcohol and the formation of dry towns and cities) across Britain and America. In Scotland, local communities were given the opportunity to vote on whether they wanted their particular town to proscribe the consumption and selling of whisky, gin, wine, or beer—and many did. Across the country, temperance halls and bars opened up serving only non-alcoholic beverages (indeed, my own great-great uncle ran such an establishment in Dunkeld). Eventually, the cause reached the corridors of power, and several legislations were brought into effect to temper the consumption of drink. Taxes were also levied on gin production and selling, effectively closing down the dens and putting Mother's Ruin beyond the reach of its target market. That market, of course, thirsty as always, turned to a drink not being targeted in this way (as it had become the drink of those making the laws)— Scotch. So, while the blenders were producing their high-quality stuff for the rich, they flooded the poor with their run-of-the-mill product. It was an instant success, and the whisky barons continued to flourish. Dark clouds, however, were looming on the horizon.

Following the assassination in Sarajevo of the Archduke Franz-Ferdinand of Austro-Hungary in June 1914, Europe spiraled out of control and descended into the chaos and carnage of the First World War. It was a conflict like no other, resulting in the pointless death of millions; and by the end, in

1918, the old order of European empires and rule had been swept away in a bloodbath of unimaginable proportions.

Britain had entered the war as the richest and most powerful nation in the world, sitting at the apex of an empire that covered nearly a quarter of the globe; but by the end it was all but ruined, and its production and wealth eclipsed by the one nation that truly benefited from Europe's implosion: the United States. However, the UK would retain her monarchy, her parliamentary institutions, and a consistency in the fabric of society, so that on the surface it was business as usual—and she fared far better than realms on the continent. However, a sea change had occurred, both at home and in her imperial reach abroad. During the war, the Prime Minister, David Lloyd George, had looked not only to win the conflict swiftly, but to do so without draining the treasury and maintaining Britain's prestige. He was also a gruff Welshman who viewed alcohol consumption as a major obstacle in achieving that aim.

As a result, and using special war-time powers, he did everything he could short of outlawing whisky to retard national consumption. Taxes were raised by nearly 500 percent, regulations were introduced to limit availability through shops or bars, and most importantly for our story, he instigated a rule that spirit must spend at least three years in an oak barrel before it could be legally sold as Scotch. It wasn't Lloyd George's intention to improve the quality of the whisky by having it mature for a minimum time, but to take three years' worth of spirit off the market at a stroke. It would be an unintentional consequence that, in trying to break our love of whisky, irrevocably improved the product, and thus, made it ultimately even more popular.

Temperance movements, abolitionist committees, and even government intervention barely dented the consumption of alcohol in the UK and across the British Empire; but across the pond in America, the movement would be taken to the ultimate conclusion, the results of which would have dramatic consequences both for Scotch and her sister spirit, bourbon.

Following the end of the war, there was an increasing demand for the US Government to do something about violent and organized crime, domestic abuse, and the nation's dependence on booze. So, in 1919, following decades of pushing by the Anti-Saloon League, and through a raft of war restrictions, the United States passed the Eighteenth Amendment to the Constitution, which at a stroke outlawed the making and selling of alcohol (although the actual drinking was not illegal in itself). It was known as Prohibition, and it was the greatest nonsense ever imposed on the American people—and ultimately, futile.

People, of course, didn't stop drinking; and prescriptions could be issued by doctors for "medicinal" alcohol. At its height, around a million of these scripts were being issued nationally every month. It was also a boon time for the smugglers, and thus provided fuel for gangs, mobsters, and organized crime. Prohibition may have cut certain types of crime, such as domestic abuse and street brawling, but it was an incredible opportunity for the likes of Al Capone to make millions and run cities like Chicago almost as a personal fiefdom, and ironically prosper under the Eighteenth Amendment and the Volstead Act that followed.

That said, ordinary working Americans obviously didn't orbit in the same world as the gangsters, but by hook or by crook strove to get a drink or two here and there. As well as doctors' notes, there was bootleg grog on a black market, and a raft of inventive ways to hide bars known as speakeasies. Like the cat and mouse world of the eighteenth century Scottish Highlands, this rage against the machine would in decades to come present a far from real romantic image of the age. There were social changes though. For the first time, women—mainly younger women—began to hang out in the new dens of eniquity, known as speakeasies, and a sort of equality, if not outright emancipation (at least in drinking habits), evolved. A new demographic would have to be catered to in the years and decades ahead.

To the Scotch industry, Prohibition brought a mixed bag of consequences: but for bourbon, America's homegrown whiskey, it was an unmitigated disaster. Up until the First World War there were scores of distilleries, large and small, across Kentucky, Tennessee, and a myriad of other states, including Illinois and West Virginia. By the time of the repeal, only a handful of distilleries, remained. It was the proscription on the production of alcohol that all but decimated the bourbon industry and very nearly wiped it off the map completely. As with the collapse in the availability of cognac half a century earlier, Scotch was quick to fill the void; but there were also some crafty characters out there with true vision as well.

Tommy Dewar was one of those truly larger-than-life figures; and along with his brother John would come to dominate much of the world of whisky, especially in the United States in the first half of the twentieth century. Their father, another John, had come from a small farm near the town of Aberfeldy in the Scottish Highlands (where he would build the first distillery custom-built for blending), but his sons would reach high office, both in Scotland and in London. Such was the power of the whisky barons.

Tommy saw the future of whisky as an unending opportunity of promoting to thirsty markets spead across the globe; and as marketer, salesman, and raconteur he travelled to nearly thirty countries spreading the gospel according to Dewar's.

Today we'd call him a Brand Ambassador, but back then it was revolutionary. Above all America was seen as fertile ground for promoting Scotch. The problem was Prohibition; but it was far from insurmountable. The United States' vast borders were as watertight as a sieve. Millions of gallons of booze flooded through from Canada and the Caribbean, with reputations made and lost along the way. This was the age of the Real McCoy. The barons took full advantage, and those Scotches that made it through filled a gap and would become household names. It was the beginning of a beautiful and lasting relationship.

Initially, Scotch sales dipped, but those companies that had built a solid base, owned several distilleries and ran a major commercial enterprise, had the capital, patience, strong home market base, and skills on board not only to ride out Prohibition, but capitalize on it (and, of course, be in a strong place at its inevitable end). Smaller, independent businesses and producers were hit hard however, and following a purge of distillers during the war, another swathe would be culled from the landscape and disappear.

It was a mark of things to come. Scores of distilleries vanished thanks to both Prohibition and war measures, such as those in Campeltown. But those left behind—a hundred or so—were the cherry-picked cream of the crop, chosen for their unique qualities and above all, blendability. The standard of production had never been so good, the whisky never better, and the commercial viability, sound. The trade-off was, of course, that virtually all distilleries, and thus the entire industry, now lay in the hands of a few companies and ruthless businessmen. Yet, this in a way saved it, as Irish and bourbon whiskies went to the wall: not set up the same or with such financial clout behind them, they withered on the vine as the tempest lashed. In the vacuum, Scotch just got stronger.

The failure of American whiskey is obvious, thanks to Prohibition; the decline of Irish whiskey is more subtle. In 1800, it dominated the whisky world, by 1900 it was sinking, and by the 1970s it looked dead and buried. The investment was still into the merchants, but those merchants not being able to control and manage the quality of that supply was failure number one. A scathing opinion of the Coffey still was number two, and the lack of genuine entrepreneurs killed it. Today, however, the Irish whiskey industry has started to rebound in a way no one would have expected a couple decades ago. At the time of writing, there are eighteen distilleries on the Emerald Isle (there were but two in the

1970s); and probably by the time you open this page, a half-dozen more have probably been added to the pantheon. It is one of the most exciting and fastest growing spirit categories on earth, but it does still have a long way to go.

After the Wall Street Crash of 1929 and the subsequent Great Depression, Prohibition (and let's face it, once you've lost everything, you need a drink) became increasingly unpopular across all strata of society, and the abolitionists more marginalized. Crime was also rampant, with Capone himself raking in over sixty million dollars in revenue without paying a dime of tax (he would go to jail for evasion). The new president, the genial Franklin Roosevelt, facing national bankruptcy understood that these tax returns were key to kick-starting the economy. With the support of another heavy hitter in New York, Mayor La Guardia, FDR was able to push the Twenty-first Amendment through Congress; and in December 1933, Prohibition was abolished. It was the first and only time that an amendment to the US Constitution was repealed. Incedently, the third is the only that has never been contested.

Times were tough globally, and while Europe fell increasingly under the thrall of various dictators and Britain struggled to maintain her vast Empire, the United States staggered through the worst economic depression in history. Yet, and almost predictably, following Prohibition, drink sales skyrocketed. The Dewar brothers and others had been effectively stockpiling for the day when the nonsense of Prohibition was revoked, and they flooded the market. And it was a sellers' market, too—well, for Scotch anyway, as there simply wasn't enough bourbon or Irish whiskey available. It was the only gig in town, and the Americans lapped it up like mother's milk. It is no coincidence that Dewar's White Label was the biggest seller in the States through the whole of the twentieth century. It was a lesson in marketing and unparalleled in an age when virtually every other domestic drinks industry was going down the drain.

The British Empire may have reached its zenith in the years following the First World War, but it was creaking; an unretainable luxury that would eventually collapse after the Second World War. Saying that, during the interwar years it still provided an opportunity for emigrants, entrepreneurs, and the whisky industry. The Scots were ever an enterprising people (a product of coming from a poor country historically) and in Australia, Canada, New Zealand, India, and from the Cape to Cairo, Scotch whisky was found in every bar and most drinks cabinets. Blended whisky had become a truly global commodity. Malt whiskies by contrast were now little more than a means to an end in the blending process, and rarely were they found bottled and sold out with their own locale.

Europeans weren't doing too great though. The dictatorships were creating drink monopolies—Franco insisted the Spanish drank Spanish wine, Mussolini the same in Italy, and so on—and as war loomed, these impositions became increasingly nationalistic and draconian. Scotch was still available, but as a luxury item or a novelty in a bar. The war itself would have severe implications as the shadow of the Nazi regime cast itself over a downtrodden continent.

Winston Churchill, who became Prime Minister in 1940 as Britain faced her darkest hour, was a very different beast to David Lloyd George. Unlike the puritanical Welshman, Churchill was a man who liked a drink and favored a Scotch and cigar above all other vices. But he was also a visionary: much as he loved the Empire and was in total denial over its imminent end, he knew that the largest sovereign entity on earth would finish the war all but bankrupt. Building for the future, he saw whisky's role in the balance of international payments as a genuinely important part of Britain's post war recovery. Thus, he did not increase taxes on whisky making (he did tax bread making), but he severely rationed its sale in order to reserve stocks.

And it was a stroke of genius. Following the Allied victory over the dark forces of Nazi Germany in 1945, the whole of Western Europe, from Scandinavia to Sicily, was an open market (in due course Eastern Europe would open up as well, and the oligarchs would swap vodka for the good stuff). By now the age of the barons had given way to new corporate giants as the industry continued to consolidate into ever-bigger concerns. There was Highland Distillers, Arthur Bell and Sons, and the Distillers Company, and as they became increasingly multinational, boardrooms would be found in London, Canada, and the United States.

The whisky barons had laid down the foundations for a remarkably enduring product, and one that would weather the storms of two world wars and Prohibition not only stonger than their rivals but emerge as the preeminent global spirit. There was luck, timing, and hard work—but the right men in the right place doing the right things turned a parochial endeavor to superstardom. Great things still lay ahead, but the road was often bumpy and not without unexpected turns.

Like many other British industries following the war and the penury of rationing, whisky boomed through the 50s and 60s; but changes were afoot. The 1960s saw massive social upheaval, a revolutionary time that spawned a new generation of drinkers more curious and with more disposable income than their fathers, and they went off on the hunt. It's also true that most of the big companies had begun to sit on their laurels, smoking big cigars in time-warped offices that looked like something out of a Dickens novel. Whisky was becoming anachronistic as a business; it was about to become so as a product. By the 70s, in Scotland at least, it had started to evolve into an old man's drink. It is arguable that it always fitted an older male demographic, and that was the target market for over half a century, but a new target audience simply passed it by as it filled new, funky bars and clubs drinking vodka, wine, and lager.

The industry was slow to react to this sea change in the market; their traditional customer base was still there drinking away, but they didn't spend as much as younger drinkers did, and they were aging and slowly dying off: hubris was killing the industry. However, it was not all doom-and-gloom, and a seed planted in the northeast would change virtually all brands and distilleries going forward: tourism.

Facing extinction, Speyside producers William Grant and Sons took an unprecedented move with their Glenfiddich distillery. First of all, in 1957 they introduced the triangle-shaped bottle, which meant it stood out on the shelf and of course resulted in more bottles able to be packed into a box, which reduced transport costs per unit. They then opened a visitor center to allow tourists to the area a chance to see inside a malt whisky distillery for the first time, and then of course "exit through the shop." It was a visionary shift—let's promote the malt we make rather than the blends it feeds. Other companies were way behind the curve on this, as they didn't realize that appreciation of the malt and where it came from could be the greatest advertising trick to promote those selfsame blends. It is no coincidence that Glenfiddich, even today, accounts for nearly a third of all malt sold—although that is fast being eroded as a new dawn rises.

The advent of the motorcar revolutionized travel in the Highlands, but it wasn't until the relative boom years following the wartime austerity that full advantage was taken by day-trippers and holidaymakers alike. Through the 1960s new motorways were being driven across England, joining together, and yet at the same time bypassing, the great industrial cities of the south; in due course these roads stretched northward to Scotland. At the same time, Scotland's principal arteries were being built, linking Edinburgh to Glasgow and Stirling, and north toward Perth, over the impressive Forth Road Bridge, completed in 1964, which was at the time the longest suspension bridge in Europe. Thomas Telford's great "Cart Track," the winding A74 connecting Glasgow with Carlisle, and more importantly joining the M6 from London, was slowly rebuilt and turned into a six-lane highway by the 1990s. In all, the vast population of the Scottish Central Belt was connected to the English south—and north came the tourists.

There was still a snag. North of Perth, the roads were abysmal as they wound like spaghetti lethargically into the Highlands or along the North Sea coast to Aberdeen; and it took an age to get to Inverness, never mind the remote corners of the country like Sutherland or Skye, where little had changed since the Victorian age. However, the UK's entry into the European Economic Community in 1973, coupled with the discovery of oil off the northeast coast, saw money pour into infrastructure projects in the Highlands, including the huge reconstruction of the Great North Road, the A9, the principal artery through the mountains and arguably the largest engineering project ever seen in the Highlands. At the timing of writing, the latest upgrade of this vital route is underway which will further facilitate the road haulage potential for the whisky producers, especially in Speyside and Easter Ross. The A96 between Aberdeen and Inverness is slowly but surely being improved, and along with the new Aberdeen by-pass should also benefit the world of whisky in the northeast.

Over the course of the 1980s and 1990s the road network in the north was transformed to the point where traveling would be unrecognizable to even the previous generation. It brought millions of visitors into a land steeped in history and lore amid a backdrop of outstanding natural beauty. Tourist boards shifted into top gear, and the whole region's economy was reconfigured toward catering to visitors. The whisky industry was not slow to jump on this bandwagon, and it couldn't have come at a better time.

Sales in Scotch were plummeting, distilleries were closing at a rate not seen since the First World War, and even some of the medium-sized players, such as Matthew Gloag and Sons or John Dewar, were swallowed up by the larger conglomerates with fingers in more pies than just whisky; a process that continues to this day. The Distillers Company, founded in 1877, was acquired by Guinness in 1986, and a year later merged with Arthur Bell & Sons, also owned by Guinness, to create United Distillers. In 1997, Guinness merged with Grand Metropolitan to form Diageo. This is in no way unique—old names once bought over by others that in turn became part of even bigger entities.

As companies merged and the industry became run by fewer and fewer boardrooms, and unprofitable or surplus distilleries closed (seventeen distilleries closed in the 1980s and seven in the 1990s), distillers began to release more and more of their line extensions (that means more than one whisky on the shelf from one company) to the market and package them in ranges like United Distillers' Classic Malts. Until around twenty years ago, most bars in Scotland, and certainly around the world, would probably have had a bottle of Glenfiddich and maybe Glenmorangie or Macallan behind the counter, but precious little else. A sea change was about to hit the whisky industry, and in its darkest hour it would be brought back to life.

No one really knows, and there are probably multiple reasons, why malt whisky drinking suddenly took off. Tourism may have played a part in making the names more familiar or sparked an interest in Scotland's homegrown drink industry and how it's made at a grassroots level. Or perhaps a generation that had experimented and explored wines, beers, and more exotic spirits came home and were curious to try malts and experience the variations of regionality and process. Also, as the ownership of the distilleries took on an increasingly global profile, CEOs wanted to use their portfolio of brands to expose the market to what they had to offer, and use the malts to a certain extent as gateways to promote the blends. The multinationals blazed a trail that the smaller independents followed. Perhaps all the elements just came together at the perfect time. Just as whisky may well have been coming out of its coma naturally, and as oft times before, the wheel of fortune turned, and whisky came back into vogue.

Seemingly overnight, the old favorites on the back bar were joined by some new faces. Along with the Diageo classics like Talisker and Lagavuillin, there were Balvenies, Glenlivets, Juras, Bowmores, and many more now familiar brands. But then the tail started wagging the dog. As the West entered an economic boom at the end of the 90s, for people with disposable incomes or curious minds, malt whisky garnered a new status. Soon, previously unknown brands appeared in household drinking cabinets, liquor stores and eventually local watering-holes. Whisky clubs appeared in Britain, Europe, and America, new magazines and books were published which enivitably drew in freelance writers and "experts." A whole symbiotic industry was born. Whisky was rising, but now the market was driving it forward, and as it became increasingly knowledgeable, the consumer demanded more variety and quality in their choice of dram.

Fueled by this, and swept up in a whirlwind not entirely of its own making (and one that took on Goliath proportions as new markets in China, the Far East, and South America opened up), distillers went into overdrive to meet the demand, increasing the number of batches possible per month to maximum capacity. New expressions arrived on the market aiming to appeal to aficionados and novices alike: double casking, sherry finishing, cask strength, and so on, all there to pander a little to the novelty element, and thus stay one step ahead of the competition in securing the loyalty of the customer base. But that base was now fluid. Whereas our grandfathers drank Bell's or Dewar's, or maybe Chivas if they felt flush, religiously, we don't—our loyalty is to quality and flavor rather than the label. The trick for the companies is to stay ahead of that curve—it meant a lot was thrown against a wall to see what would stick.

This Big Bang of whisky release only saw quality rise, and with it all the tools of the trade. Brand Ambassadors, specialist tastings, and educational programs all emerged to guide, escort, and provide a route map through the wonderful world of whisky. This is still evolving, and new technologies are constantly being developed and adapted to serve the modern whisky barons: the grandiose chairmen in London, New York, Tokyo, or even India who oversee the biggest spirits industry on earth.

CHAPTER 2

MOTHER TONGUES

Is fheàrr Gàidhlig bhriste na Gàidhlig sa chiste.
It is better to have broken Gaelic than no Gaelic.
—Old Highland proverb

Twelve hundred years ago there were six languages in common currency in what today we would call Scotland: Gaelic, Welsh, Anglo-Saxon (English), Pictish (akin to Welsh, but with unknown ancient roots), Norse, and Latin. Each has their own tale to tell, and each has left an indelible mark on the etymological map of Scotland—and consequently on the names of her distilleries.

Back then there were no countries or nations as such, but a patchwork of kingdoms and fiefdoms, where strongmen and robber barons contested the spoils of the land. As noted, we think of Scotland as a country less productive agriculturally than say, England or France, but with a population of around 750,000 the available land was more than sufficient to support a pretty well organized social order within each of these rival domains. War was ever present, but in those far off days, that was the norm across Europe, and Scotland was no exception. In fact, Scotland was fairly unique in that it coalesced into a coherent country (albeit not a nation state as we'd understand it today) hundreds of years before her continental cousins. When modern England appeared as a country following the Norman Conquest in 1066 a united Scotland was already two hundred years old and the dominant player in the British Isles.

Most anthropologists and linguists agree that the Basque language is not only unique but very ancient. Claims that it may well be the language (or at least a common descendant) of the people who painted the caves of Luscerne and Cro Magnon 40,000 years ago are probably exaggerated, but it is old—very old—and the last remnant of a time when hundreds of independent language families crisscrossed Europe. "Eenie, meenie, miny, mo"—a common schoolyard rhyme—is actually believed to be a "one, two, three, four" fossil of some long-lost language. These are tantalizing windows into a different linguistic heritage.

All modern Western European languages are Indo-European; that is, they share a commonality and the same root origin—somewhere in the Asiatic Steppe. Whether you speak German or Welsh, Catalan or Swedish, it's all Indo-European. Except Basque. The Celtic languages of Britain (Welsh, Gaelic of Ireland, and the Gaelic of Scotland) are themselves antique tongues, prehistoric; but they are still part of the family.

The name Celtic is a relatively modern term, essentially coined by a Welsh linguist in the nineteenth century to clump the Welsh and Gaelic groups of languages into a family; which was then broken down further into P-Celtic (Welsh, Breton, and Cornish) and Q-Celtic (Gaelic and Manx, derived from the phonetic sound made at the end of the word for son: ma**p** in Welsh, ma**c** in Gaelic). The two groups share a commonality for sure, but also one of culture, art, and music. And this culture was very similar to, and indeed is probably a relic of, a diverse group of peoples living in northwestern and central Europe around two thousand years ago. The Romans referred to them in a sweeping generalization as Barbarians, the Greeks called them *Keltoi*, which means "Secret People"—a reference to their non-written oral traditions. And from this we get Celtic. But let's have no misunderstanding: people living in Ireland or the Scottish Highlands a thousand years ago would neither have called themselves Celts or even known what one was.

With that caveat in mind, the two "Celtic" language groups came into Scotland independently of each other and left very different legacies.

There was for a long time a raging debate on whether there was a mass migration of Celts into the British Isles at a point in antiquity, or whether there were a few incomers with a superior technology that the locals adopted, and slowly, the cultural aspect changed as a result. DNA study and archeology has pretty much cleared this up—there was no mass movement of people from the near continent, but an influx of better tools and farming equipment, mastery of the horse, and the introduction of iron around 700 BC. The linga franca of this revolution were the Q-Celtic Gaelic languages, probably hailing from northern Spain, and within a short space of time these Gaelic-family languages were spoken the length and breadth of the British Isles (possibly arriving via Ireland), replacing the old indigenous non-Indo European tongues that may well have their roots going back to the Ice Age—and whose only fragments are left to us in some river names.

Social order changed, too; things became less communal (the practice of erecting standing stones or constructing elaborate tombs for example: although this had begun to change anyway) and more confrontational. A deteriorating climate, with the weather turning colder and wetter (the treeline in Scotland plummeted) probably augmented the original movement of technology, and with a desire to protect less and less usable land this precipitated the development of a warrior society with kings and warlords at the apex. The ready adoption of horses and iron can be better understood against this backdrop—and likely there was prestige and rank associated with these new ways, too. Old religions may have crumbled as well, giving way to a new pantheon of Celtic gods and practices of worship (we retain some of this in old festivals, such as Halloween).

The P-Celtic languages, which seemed to have originated in the Low Countries, arrived into Britain (but not Ireland) around 500 BC, and very quickly replaced Gaelic, with the exception of Argyll and the Inner Hebridean islands, which lay somewhat isolated beyond a broad swathe of mountains. This new wave developed in the south into old Welsh and would have been the language of the peoples first encountered by the Romans. In the northeast of Scotland and throughout most of the Highlands a similar tongue emerged, but it may also have retained and incorporated elements of Gaelic, and even some earlier Neolithic tongue.

From Roman time to the present, we have referred to this group of people as the Picts, and their language, Pictish. This is likely a sort of nickname coined by the Romans guarding Hadrian's Wall and means "Painted People" (a reference to their practice of covering their bodies in tattoos or more likely woad—the blue warpaint that Mel Gibson slathered all over himself in *Braveheart*, but was no longer in practice by William Wallace's time—which is mildly hallucinogenic and very good at fending off the midgies). It was probably employed across Britain, and the root origin of the term "Britain" may be another painted reference with possible Neolithic origins, but by Roman times it seems only the Picts, locked away in their far-off hills and glens, were still actively painting themselves ahead of battles.

We have no idea what the Picts called themselves, and indeed there may not have been a collective name until very late on, by which time they may have adopted the term to describe themselves as a whole. I think each tribe simply went by the name of their own region or kingdom (Caledonia, a Latin corruption of an actual sub-kingdom in the southern Highlands, would be an obvious example). We also have little written evidence for their language either, but from place names and king-lists historians have inferred a lot about this most enigmatic of people and their tongue.

The Pictish realms fifteen hundred years ago stretched from the Forth Coast all the way to the northern tip of the country, offshore to the northern isles of Orkney and Shetland, and west to the Outer Hebrides. South of the wide River Forth, the Anglo-Saxon kingdom of Northumbria held domain over a diverse group of peoples, some Celtic and some (increasingly) English. To the west, south of Loch Lomond and reaching all the way to the beautiful hills of the

Lake District, was a territory that would emerge into history as Strathclyde, a Welsh speaking region that would exist as an independent kingdom until the eleventh century.

Across the hills to the west was Dalriada, a Gaelic speaking kingdom with strong social and cultural ties to Ireland, a mere twelve miles away. Dalriada was truly a sea kingdom. Probably administered from the Island of Islay, strategically positioned halfway between Scotland and Ireland, and easily seen from both mainlands, their spiritual heart and the site of royal coronations was on Dunadd Hill in Mid Argyll, about thirty miles south of Oban. Yet for all of their maritime might, by the eighth century the Gaels of Dalriada were to all intents and purposes ruled by the Pictish kings far over the mountains in Perthshire, or at times up the Great Glen near Inverness. But things were about to change dramatically and without warning.

Figure 2.1 Lagavulin sign

A new and irresistible force from the north arrived like bolt of lightening in 793 when a Viking host, fresh from the deep fjords of Norway descended upon the undefended island of Lindisfarne off the coast of Northumbria near Berwick-upon-Tweed, in what is now England. Two years later they raided and ransacked the holy sanctuary on the sacred Isle of Iona in the heart of Dalriada's sea kingdom. The Gaelic realm in the west was crumbling. A joint effort by the Picts, Gaels, and even the warriors of Strathclyde could not stave them off. By the ninth century all of the islands of the coast of Scotland were under the cosh of Norse rule; and a fair amount of the mainland, too, especially in the north and in Argyll.

In 839, a joint Gaelic/Pictish army was annihilated by a Viking force somewhere in the region of the Ochil Hills, north and west of Edinburgh, and it would have far reaching consequences for the development of Scotland. The old regime was blown away, paving the way for an opportunistic warlord who was in the right place at the right time when the dice fell.

His name was Kenneth MacAlpine, and in 853 he became joint king of both Pictland and Dalriada; and Christened his new realm Alba. Pronounced "ah-la-ba," this is still the Gaelic name for Scotland, and the word is rooted in an ancient term for "white" (albino has the same origins), and may refer to the white clouds that seem to always cover our fair land, or more likely to the White Cliffs of Dover (MacAlpine's Alba was a borrowed term from the Irish name for the whole island of Great Britain, but by the ninth century had been truncated to apply to Scotland alone, although England retains the romantic term of Albion's Plain).

MacAlpine became Kenneth I, and all subsequent kings and queens of Scotland and Britain draw their regnal number from him (and from William I in the English line). In the decades and centuries that followed, contest for the throne was bitter and bloody. Few kings sat for long. MacAlpine's grandsons were sent to Ireland for their protection as boys, and when they returned to claim the crown they brought the old Gaelic language back with them (this probably saw the rise of several Dalriadic lords, who had been out of favor in the Pictish-dominated court at Scone); and in time—and for many diverse reasons, this being chief though—all of Scotland north of the Forth and Clyde rivers would end up speaking Gaelic, and certainly by 1000, Pictish was gone. Its vanishing remains yet another unsolved mystery in the story of Scotland.

Many modern Scottish lordships and earldoms emerged in this period—inheritances of previous Pictish regions no doubt, but now carrying almost exclusively Gaelic names. These names paint a picture of Scottish geography and history over a thousand years ago. In addition, looking at any Ordnance Survey map, you can peel back the layers of time by investigating the names of rivers, hills, and old settlements. It describes the fluid nature of the language changes that took place in the years between 900 and 1400, with some purely of Gaelic origin, some Pictish, Norse, English, Welsh, and of course, some a mix of each. In no small measure our distillery names, often drawn from older settlements, would come to reflect this, inheritied from their place on the map and the country around them.

South of the Forth-Clyde line, place names and regions are mostly of Welsh or English origins in the main (there is some Gaelic, especially in the southwest area of Galloway)—Glasgow (Welsh origin) and Edinburgh (English-Gaelic) are the most obvious examples. And in the far north, and especially the Northern Isles, the influence of Norse is everywhere, with virtually all place names on Orkney and Shetland of Viking derivation.

These languages have woven a patchwork quilt across our land, threaded and colorful as a home-spun kilt: deeply connected with our long, bloody, and diverse history. Today, all but a few Scots speak only English, which can be both a simple language and a frustratingly complex one at the same time. With root words borrowed from nearly thirty European tongues and a giant vocabulary and unique grammar that can be baffling to the learner. The victory of the English language is in its versatility and adaptability. It has also piggybacked on two of the most powerful political entities to have existed—the British Empire and the United States—and stretches its reach around the world like no other. It takes no prisoners, and looking forward, it is hard not to see many other European languages fading away, as Gaelic and Welsh before them, against the onslaught. Yet it was in Europe that English was born.

Old English evolved out of a very early form of Frisian, once spoken in that corner of the North Sea coast from Holland, through Germany, to southern Denmark. Modern Dutch borrows much from this maritime Germanic tongue.

If you sit in a Frisian bar and just listen to the tone and timbre of the conversations around you, it will sound alien of course, but at the same time oddly familiar. And it was from this rather rustic homeland that a global language would emerge.

Toward the end of the Roman occupation of the southern half of Britain, the administration had to increasingly rely on mercenaries from all corners of the empire—Italian soldiers were simply in too short a supply as outside pressures threatened to destroy the imperial fabric totally. Inscriptions, graffiti if you prefer, on "The Wall" show a diverse ethnic mix, most coming from places far warmer and sunnier than the hills of northern England. A rich source of men and materials was the near continent, and so thousands of Germanic soldiers were shipped across the narrow channel between the Low Countries and East Anglia or Kent. Collectively, we tend today to clump them into a group called the Anglo-Saxons; but in truth, they came from a variety of tribal units, with three principals: the Angles (from the corner of Denmark and Germany), who would give their name to the country they came to (Angle-land = England); the Saxons from Saxony; and the Jutes from Jutland (northern Denmark).

When the Romans finally left in 420, law and order effectively broke down, and the now-unpaid Germanic warriors with fire in their bellies and swords in their hands were no match for the local and largely gentrified or civilized Celtic Britons. The jury is out on whether there was wholesale genocide, intermarriage, or a piecemeal military advance (probably a mix of all three as there is significant evidence that a local aristocracy maintained at least some level of privilege). Anglo-Saxons (which by the eighth century was the accepted name for the original English group), reinforced by large numbers of their kinsmen flooding in from the continent, had overrun all of east, central, and southern England (the Angles in the north, the Saxons in the central area, London and the southwest, and the Jutes in Kent and part of the south coast).

The British fought back (stories of Arthur probably originate from this time), but it was always a rearguard action as the English kept coming. In time, the Goddodin of Lothian in southern Scotland would be defeated and overwhelmed by the Northumbrian Angles who occupied Edinburgh, and with vaulting ambition would continue a conquest north until finally stopped just north of Dundee near Forfar in 683. They would consolidate their hold on the southeastern corner of Scotland until 1016, when King Malcolm II finally defeated them on the River Tweed and moved the border of Alba south to where it lies today.

In the southern half of the island, the English pushed the Britons into the wild mountains and forests of the west—the old Anglo-Saxon word for foreigner is *Welisċ* and is where the words Wales and Welsh come from. Here in Wales the English were halted, and for a time the Cornish penisular too (Cornwall means the Horn of Wales in Old English). The Saxons would be back.

The near five hundred years of Northumbrian English rule in southeast Scotland left an indelible mark, not just in place names, but in dialect and speech. The subsequent thousand years of Scottish rule have meant that today the accent shift from the Scottish Borders into Northumberland on crossing the Tweed is marked and noticeable; it wasn't always the case. When the monk, the Venerable Bede, was writing his history of the Anglo-Saxons in the eighth century there would have been little distinction at all. It is the artificial erecting of the border that has created the dialect shift because on both sides of it are simply variations on the same Old English language theme; both are dialects of English.

In 1070, the Scottish king, Malcolm III married Margaret of Wessex (a corruption of West Saxon), sister to Edgar Ætheling, the Royal House of Wessex's pretender to the English throne following the successful invasion of William of Normandy in 1066. The future Saint Margaret, as she would eventually in death become, is famous for her charitable work, establishing of monasteries and abbeys, and for her persuasive and powerful personality. She spoke a form of what by then was Middle English, which would have been easily understood by merchants, nobles, and clergymen in the Lothians, but not in the heart of the kingdom, which at that time still gravitated toward Perth, where Gaelic reigned. She would put a stop to that.

The civil servants of the medieval world were the learned clergy—monasteries and cathedrals from Canterbury to Iona were producing the most exquisite works of literary art, such as the Book of Kells and the Lindisfarne Gospels, and the monks and priests were the most literate in society (it is unlikely that Malcolm himself could read and write, although undoubtedly his devout wife did). Margaret brought her men of God north from England, and in doing so, the business of court was all but changed to English speaking, and this became the decree sent forth to the nobility by, somewhat ironically, a Gaelic speaking king. Thus, the seed was sown, but it would be their son David I who would cement the change nationwide.

The most unlikely of monarchs, David I was the third son of Malcolm III, and for much of his youth had lived in Norman England, fleeing into exile as his uncle Donald Ban seized power. He lived the life of luxury and when his sister, Matilda, married the English king, Henry I, his position at court would have become most significant. Still, he was a minor royal—albeit a clever and astute one. He watched and learned the Norman system of kingly rule well and began to understand how real royal power could be exercised (this against a backdrop of centuries of Scottish kings being murdered or killed in battle by their successors or the nobility). This was a new operation, and David was a keen student.

In 1124, after the death of his two elder and childless brothers, astonishingly David inherited the throne of Alba. He would rule a complex and war-torn nation for thirty years, which was a staggeringly long time in those days. He would push her boundaries to the gates of York, and his institutions influence Scotland to this day.

David had seen the feudal system first-hand—a truly powerful blunt instrument of authority—and he spent no little time introducing it into Celtic Scotland. Feudalism meant a lot more than a pyramid system which saw the king at the top and power trickled down through lords and knights to peasants. In addition, it meant a fundamental rearrangement of clerical appointments, the formalizing of a functioning bureaucracy, and above all, the establishment of Royal Burghs—towns with special trading privileges and local authority over an agricultural hinterland. Every part of daily life, every aspect of the secular and the spiritual now had a hierarchy, and at the top was the king (well, technically the Pope—but he was far, far away). The language of this new system was a newly emerging form of English: Anglo-Norman—essentially a Germanic tongue peppered with French.

As perhaps it was with Gaelic and Welsh sixteen hundred years earlier, it was commerce and technology that forced a population that relied on subsistence farming, market prices, and the good graces of the castle lords to adopt English as the spoken language in order to feed themselves and their families—at least in southern and eastern Scotland (where the Royal Burgh's were established). When David I ascended the throne, few areas of Scotland geographically were English speaking, just the Lothian and Border enclave; within a couple of generations it was spoken by all south of the Highlands, save a few pockets in Galloway. Not withstanding, higher classes did speak Norman-English or Latin.

What would become the English dialect spoken in Scotland, Broad Scots or Lallans evolved from this Middle English/Norman brogue (David would bring knights and barons north to help execute his fledgling system). Many common names like Stewart, Bruce, Murray, Gordon, Menzies, Grant and so on are the descendants of these new arrivals. There are those who say that Scots is a distinct language; spend any time in rural Aberdeenshire and you might just think that. But looking at its development, it is hard to agree. Scots as spoken by Robert Burns for example in the eighteenth century is more of a time capsule: a snapshot of the way everyone spoke in both the north of England and the south of Scotland nearly five hundred years ago. There is no such thing as perfect English, which is a consequence of its coherent flexibility—it doesn't have to conform to a norm to be fully understood; and in a country like Scotland, that has left a mark just as diverse as Gaelic. That flexibility has undoubtly contributed to its global success.

The road to English domination in the Highlands and the Hebrides has come at the cost of the Gaelic language. There are numerous reasons for this: from the Statutes of Iona to the Highland Clearances, and a long persecution of Gaelic by Lowland authorities. Gaelic also was late in producing a common Bible, which meant that people had to read English to understand the written word. The 1872 Education Act meant that lessons could no longer be taught in Gaelic, and indeed many schools enforced a Gaelic Free policy, especially in the southern and eastern Highlands.

These areas had also been opened up during the nineteenth century by improvements in road and rail, and with increased commerce came an increased usage of English. The decline initially was slow, but with so many young men going off to fight in the First World War and having to speak English to get anywhere, coupled with the education policies of the early twentieth century, great numbers of Highlanders were simply switched off, and the decline fell off the cliff. There was also an almost self-imposed stigma attached, too (one borne of decades of being told Gaelic was backward); and that generation was determined not to have that visited on their children. So, in a self-fulfilling prophecy, Gaels often refused to speak Gaelic at home and emphasized the importance of speaking English.

The decline of the language in the twentieth century has been rapid, with a loss of 10 to 20 percent of native speakers every census. There are no monoglots (people who can only speak Gaelic) left, and in areas like Perthshire or Aberdeenshire the native dialect has vanished within my own lifetime. Only really in the Isles and in pockets of the western Mainland does the language cling on. In reality, only in the Outer Hebrides, north and west Skye, Tiree, and southwest Islay is it spoken regularly. Today, there are around fifty thousand native speakers—approximately 1.1 percent of the Scottish population. English is master in the north, but the geography and the place names hide the truth that this transformation is recent. And when we look at the names of the distilleries and the single malts made there, few are English language in origin. Instead they all reflect our once diverse rainbow of mother tongues.

CHAPTER 3

FOR THESE ARE MY MOUNTAINS AND THESE ARE MY GLENS

An nì a thig leis a'ghaoith, falbhaidh e leis an uisge.
What comes with the wind will go with the water.
—Gaelic proverb

The underlying fabric of Scotland is truly ancient, erected on timescales that are utterly unfathomable to the human mind. It has a geology so diverse that few countries on earth, and certainly none so small, can match the eclectic hodgepodge that underpins our landscape. This geography, and its associated climate, has played its part in the locations of the distilleries and contrived to create a land upon which many of the whiskies take their names.

Scotland is riven with faultlines; nothing quite so dramatic as say, the Anatolian or San Andreas, but rather relics of a far more violent past when the landscape was being formed, when very different looking Scotlands existed, each bequeathing us with their own indelible marks. Essentially there are four major faults: the Southern Upland Fault (Girvin in Ayrshire to Dunbar in East Lothian); the Highland Boundary Fault (Helensburgh on the Clyde to Stonehaven near Aberdeen); the Great Glen Fault (a cleft through the Highlands upon which Loch Ness and Inverness lie); and the Moine Thrust (a folding fault in the Northwest Highlands). The Southern Upland and Highland Boundary Faults mark the limits of an ancient rift valley, which today contains the bulk of Scotland's population in a low-lying country known as the Central Belt. The Great Glen cleaves the Highlands in half and is the most obvious of faults on any map of the country—or more spectacularly from space these days. But it is with the Moine Thrust that this story begins.

Essentially, continental crust is lighter than oceanic crust, and these islands or plates of rock float around on a sea of molten magma, often crashing into each other, building mountain ranges, sometimes tearing apart to make new oceans. This has been going on since the dawn of time. The original building blocks of our continents are known as cratons, which formed when the surface of the earth was still a bubbling fireball around four billion years ago. They form the heart of every modern landmass, and in Europe, Scandinavia is the principal craton (Western Europe has no such base); and in North America, the great Canadian Shield and most of Greenland are built of these truly primeval rocks.

Around 430 million years ago a continent roughly equating to modern day Europe collided head-on with North America, throwing up a vast mountain range as high as the Himalayas and as long, known as the Caledonian Orogeny. As Europe ploughed on, it folded up its own rock layers and then thrust them over the incoming North American plate. Then around one hundred twenty million years ago, with these great mountains worn down to stumps, the two landmasses broke apart, opening the Atlantic Ocean. However, the split wasn't along the original line of contact, but several hundred miles farther west, and this left Scotland with an unusual legacy.

Running along the watershed of the Northwest Highlands is a geological shift of epic proportions: The rocks to the east of the divide are around four hundred million years old and originate from the mountain building period; to the west, the rocks are over 3.5 *billion* years old—a magnitude of nearly tenfold. What happened was this: as the Atlantic opened, a sliver of the North American craton remained glued to the northwest of Scotland, and these now exposed Lewisian Gneiss formations are by far the oldest rocks in Europe. The result is a near lunar landscape where great singular peaks like Stac Pollaidh and Suilven rise out of a wild, barren landscape, while across the line a complex geology that sees older rocks piled up over younger rocks has generated a bizarre world of mountain and glen. It was the understanding of the Moine Thrust zone that started geologists down the path of understanding plate-tectonics as a whole.

From the Moine Thrust in the north, and west to the Highland Boundary Fault, the mountain landscape in between was erected during that Caledonian mountain building Period, and has been shaped and sculpted into one of the most beautiful landscapes in the world, the bulk of which makes up a broad range known as the Grampian Mountains. It is from these high peaks that much of the water originates for the distilleries, and they also play a large part in the climate, which in turn affects the whisky's maturation.

To further complicate the story, Scotland is tilted to the east, a result of the opening of the Atlantic and the vast forces of separation uplifting the west of the country. In doing so, huge volcanoes such as the Cuillin of Skye or those on Mull, and of famous Ailsa Craig in the Firth of Clyde erupted violently, as volcanoes continue to do today on Iceland. Consequently, all of Scotland's great rivers and river systems generally rise on the high hills in the west and run through to the North Sea in the east.

Fast flowing streams fueled by heavy rains and spring snow melt dig deep and erode the steep valleys through which they gush, creating spectacular waterfalls and cataracts before merging to form larger rivers. The rocks of the Highlands are generally hard metamorphic schists (old sedimentary rock, such as sandstone that has been heated, melted, and folded under great pressures to have their structures altered and hardened on re-solidification) or granites. This bedrock is mineral rich, and when the rivers finally reach the lower-lying country of the east, their momentum drops and they deposit these nutrient minerals, which in turn creates dark fertile soils perfect for growing the barley needed for whisky production.

The distilleries themselves require cold water, preferably snow-melt water, in order to have optimum spirit making conditions; and the fast-flowing streams coming off the uplands are perfect for this. Within the stills it is important to maintain the correct pressure, and in condensing the spirit, the preferred temperature, which cannot be achieved if it gets too warm or if the water isn't cold enough. Thus, most distilleries tend to close down during the warmest weeks of the summer in what is called the "Silent Season."

Rainfall (snow in the winter months) is not evenly distributed across Scotland, which is due in no small part to the topography of the Grampian Mountains. The prevailing winds come from the west, which is a warm and wet direction; and moisture-laden clouds and storms come rattling in from the Atlantic on something of a conveyor belt. As these low-pressure systems and fronts hit the hills of the west they dump their loads, which in turn creates a rain shadow in the east. There are places in the mountains that receive in excess of one hundred eighty inches of rain/snow a year (that's fifteen *feet* a year), and the town of Fort William which lies at the foot of Ben Nevis, Britain's highest peak, gets around one hundred fifteen inches per annum. In addition, this falls on average over the course of around two hundred sixty-five days a year. When people think of Scotland as a wet country, this is where they're thinking of, as the Western Highlands is among the wettest places in Europe. Indeed, the ancient pine woods of the west would qualify as rain forest.

Figure 3.1 Tomintoul Hills
(photo reproduced with permission of Tom Hughes)

By contrast, there are parts of the east coast around Edinburgh and north of Aberdeen where the rainfall is around 21 inches a year. That's less than Rabat, the capital of Morroco (it's also less than London, Rome, Barcelona, and Sydney, Australia). So, when people say that it always rains in Scotland, this is not where they're thinking of. Generally speaking, the Central Belt and the east coast from Berwick in the southeast round to Easter Ross (the arable land north of Inverness) is in the rain shadow, and relatively dry. The Central Highlands get a decent fall of rain and snow per year, and the west is wet. There's no hiding that truth.

To make whisky you need water, so it would seem to suggest that the west would be best, with a near constant supply foaming down the mountains. But not so—it is simply too wet and the land too soaked, with minerals leached out to sustain large-scale agriculture; and so, there was historically a dearth of available grain. In the east where the sun shines and the rivers have deposited the rich nutrients, you can grow plenty of barley, but you don't have the water to sustain industrial whisky production. Thanks to the geography and the climate it influences, it is in the happy medium where whisky can be commercially made; therefore, it is no coincidence that this plays a huge role in the geographical spread of the distilleries themselves.

The Cairngorm Mountains are a block of pink granite rising to over 4,000 feet above sea level, and their snowcapped peaks (positively spooky Ben Macdui is the highest at 4,296 feet) tower over the wide valleys of Strathspey to the north and Royal Deeside to the south. The Cairngorm plateau was formed from ancient lavas embedded in the bowels of the great mountain range. Weathering has worn the neighboring softer rock to leave these behemoths standing like sentinels in the heart of the Grampians. They dominate the east central Highlands, where the rainfall is relatively low. The bustling town of Aviemore on the banks of the Spey receives around thirty inches per annum, but the sheer presence of these hills means that on the high frozen rock-shattered plateau less than ten miles away nearly ninety inches falls (from September through May it falls as snow, allowing for viable commercial skiing on the north-facing slopes).

Gravitating around the high central plateau are other high peaks—Beinn a' Bhuird, Ben Avon, and Lochnagar to the east and south, and the Monadhliath mountains to the west. Beyond these are lower, rolling hills. And as the great white peaks give way to lower ground, the fast-flowing rivers reach into the barley-rich lands of lower Strathspey. Here two worlds meet: high volume, constant running, cold water flowing fast off the hills, and rolling arable, high yielding barley country. This is the region referred to as 'Speyside' and nearly two thirds of all distilleries are in this area. This was the potential seen by the Duke of Gordon, and as we have seen his determination fueled to a certain extent the rise of the modern whisky industry.

Other areas of distillery clustering also include Highland Perthshire and Easter Ross for much the same reasons, and historically both areas once had numerous operations. Islay is another part of the country famed for her whiskies and unique among the islands for the sheer concentration of malts. But we'll get to that.

Periodically over the course of the last two million years, Scotland has been covered by great ice sheets, some a mile thick, and most recently, 13,500 years ago. The ice returned briefly again 11,500 years ago, before melting completely 1,500 years later, ushering in the warm period we enjoy today known as the Holocene. The massive glaciers oozing out of the Highlands formed a cap that covered the whole of the northern half of Britain south to Yorkshire and beyond. As the ice retreated back into the uplands it left huge amounts of gravels, sands, and other debris behind. This would blanket the low-lying country and provide a rich source of groundwater, and in time develop into the dark soils that advanced the agricultural revolution of the eighteenth century. Scotland's rivers and streams would be borne from this de-glaciacion, and that legacy would play its own part in distillery locations.

Figure 3.2 Waterfalls Glen Etive

In Lowland Scotland, once the land was drained, the rocks removed and fashioned into the mile upon mile of stone-walled field enclosures, and small holdings replaced with larger entities, these underlying fertile soils turned the area into a breadbasket. The population exploded, inevitably furnishing the growing cities and their voracious demand for manpower in the Industrial Revolution which followed quick on the heels of this rural makeover. Profits were made, new towns built, and for those who remained, a widening diversity of enterprise emerged. Distilling had been as much a part of Lowland life as it had been in the Highlands, but it would head in a very different direction.

The Central Belt is a rift valley, caught between the Highland Boundary Fault to the north and the Southern Upland Fault to the south. The rift formed toward the end of the mountain building period, when the land stretched a little and this slice sank into the crust. Millions of years of erosion from the mountains and deposition in the Lowlands means that the once very noticeable contrast from one side of the fault to the other has been significantly diminished; but it's still there and provides not only a geological shift, but a cultural one, too. In some ways, the story of Scotland has been influenced by the differences between the Highlands and Lowlands, and in such a way our geography has shaped us.

The Central Belt stretches from the dairy farms of Ayrshire to the beef country of Angus and Kincardine and is deeply indented by the large estuaries of the Forth and Clyde rivers. It is a landscape of low green hills and gentle valleys pock-marked here and there with the remnants of a volcanic heritage as the rift formed. This area is home to the bulk of Scotland's five million people, concentrated essentially around Glasgow and Edinburgh. Geology and providence provided the raw materials and the means to reach markets that allowed the industrial heartland to thrive; and to make, in particular, the west of Scotland the "engine room" of the British Empire. These growing cities needed to be fed, watered, and indulged with alcohol (it was a grim and harsh working life—any escape would do).

As we have seen, *jenever* (gin) flourished in Flanders and Holland, and during the Eighty Years' War, when the Dutch fought for independence against their Hapsburg overlords, they were supported by English mercenaries who would take a good scoop of this juice before going into battle to settle the nerves; this is the origin of the phrase "Dutch Courage." Indeed, gin was so popular that the returning soldiers brought the methodology and the thirst back home. The Glorious Revolution of 1688-1689 saw the enthronement of William of Orange, a Dutchman, as well as a surge in demand and popularity. By the early eighteenth century there may have been nearly eight thousand gin shops in London alone.

The government's restrictions and heavy taxing of imported alcohols helped, and thus, locally made gin became the English spirit of choice (by 1730 the average Londoner was consuming over two twenty ounce pints of gin a week). However, drunkenness, crime, and the squalid nature of the gin dens was out of control as they saw it, and the lawmakers' love affair with Mother's Ruin, as it became known, was short-lived. The enacted law of 1736 (Spirits Duties Act 1735) brought in punitive taxes and led to riots. A further "Sale of Spirits Act, 1750" was more successful, and much of the unlicenced gin production was driven underground. Few new English gin licences were applied for in this period.

These acts were also accompanied by the government's mission to curtail homegrown spirit production from grains (several poor harvests and food shortages were behind much of this). Although these restrictions did not apply to whisky directly, with Scotland's differing licencing laws, many distillers in the Lowlands took advantage of shortages in England and switched to gin making. It was a lucrative industry with a thirsty audience.

Yet, toward the end of the eighteenth century consumption had begun to dwindle; the market was shrinking, and for various reasons the "gin craze" was over. Scottish producers found it harder to penetrate new opportunities, and many producers simply closed or went back to making whisky. Here, too, there was an issue for the Lowlanders.

The late eighteenth century also saw vast improvements to communications across the country—more reliable roads, bridges, new canals, and better facilities to aid the traveler. It is hard to underestimate the changes that took place, and the social reordering that followed in the years 1760 to 1820. Within a single lifetime, the very shape of farming was altered beyond recognition from what had existed for centuries before; new technology was sweeping the land and with it, diversity. The great cities blossomed within that lifetime, including the wonderful Georgian world of Edinburgh's New Town and the huge shipping on the Clyde in Glasgow. This was the Age of Reason, of Adam Smith, of James Watt, of the Enlightenment, and it changed not only how Scotland looked, but how it thought.

Scotsman Thomas Telford was the greatest engineering genius of his time; he laid the foundations of much of our modern infrastructure, from roads and harbors to churches and canals. Scotland was always a hard land to tame, especially in the north, and his new roads carved through the hills and spanned raging rivers and brought the communities of the Highlands closer than they'd ever been to the cities of the south. This was a boon to trade, but it also brought both ideas and sheep north in one of the worst excesses of social experimentation: the horrors of the Highland Clearances, and a landscape and economy utterly transformed. Indirectly, and although largely locally, whisky would play a part in this change.

The upkeep of these roads was through a mixture of toll collection and landowner subsidy, and they needed to be seen to be earning a return. Certainly, they brought consumer and producer together, and their many miles were punctuated by numerous inns and taverns. Here was a ready-made market: it was time for the water of life to leave its native glens.

With many distilleries in the south producing gin, the Highlanders found a ready audience for their quality product. It was more robust, but also seemed to be smoother and better balanced. In short, it had matured. Barrels have been used for centuries to transport all sorts of stuff, from grain to wine, and salt to sugar; they are simply perfect for the job. Coopering is an art, a magical blend of precision craftsmanship and aesthetics. As distance to markets increased, the whisky would spend longer in the cask, which had the effect of maturing it (the same thing was noticed by bourbon producers sailing their spirit on the long journey down the Mississippi to New Orleans). In time, consumers began asking for cask-aged whisky. So, once the Lowland producers came back online they faced fierce competition: but, it would be a race to the top not the bottom, and ultimately the industry thrived. Ideologically this was a benefit to the consumer; but the real winner was of course the taxman. Some things never change.

Scotland's geography and climate has had a massive role to play in the distribution of her distilleries, but the taming of that geography, the arable revolutions, the growth of the cities, and the new transport links all served to further the ends of single malt. But ultimately, it is people that have shaped the industry and made it what it is today.

CHAPTER 4

OF GODS AND MEN

"Goodnight, and may your God go with you."
—Dave Allen

The quote above is from the late, great Irish comedian, Dave Allen, who possessed an uncanny knack of taking the mundane of our daily lives and finding wonderful humor in it. His iconic pose was on a stool next to a tall, slender round table and always—and that's always—there was a glass of whisky on it. Whisky is a social drink, a universal glass of bonhomie, a dram to be shared in good times and bad with friends, companions and even enemies. But, we'd be naive to forget that at heart it is a commercial entity, and to have been so successful that a top TV entertainer would be seen as classy with a glass of it by his side took the ingenuity and brilliance of actual individuals: the men and women who helped make Scotch what it is and lent their names to so many familiar brands. And that story begins with a truly remarkable individual who lived an inconceivably long time ago.

It has long been believed that *uisge beatha* was brought from Ireland to Scotland by evangelizing monks in the Middle Ages; and there is no reason to doubt that story, for whole legions of priests and holy men came over the North Channel to preach and convert the local Gaelic and Pictish communities. The best known of these was Saint Columba (*Colm Cille* in Gaelic), who established a monastery on the small island of Iona in 563, and from where generations of monks and saints would emanate and spread the length and breadth of Scotland, setting up daughter houses from where they could seed the Word and grow the influence of the early Church.

Many of these early pioneer clerics would go on to be canonized into saints; fathers of a homegrown Celtic church, and their names are to be found the length and breadth of the nation in numerous place names. From Dunblane (Hill of Saint Blane) to Loch Maree (Loch of Saint Mael Rubha) our landscape is peppered with lakes, towns, hills, and farms dedicated to this or that saint; most of whom are completely unheard of today. The majority of these pioneers came from either Ireland, like Columba, or from the British speaking lands (Cumbria, Strathclyde, or Wales), such as Saint Patrick. Their names tend to be rendered in the local vernacular of the time, and thus more obscure to us today.

Certain priests tended to focus on specific regions—Saint Kertigan in Glasgow, Saint Machar in Aberdeen, Saint Ciaran in the southwest, and Saint Mael Rubha in the northwest. Columba himself seems to have been quite the traveler though, visiting a king in the Inverness region, and then another near Perth a hundred miles to the south. Amid all this galavanting he was also running the holy abbey of Iona.

Although Columba was quite the trailblazer, those who came after had to deal with something of a juggling act with emerging bishops appointed by Rome who had specific territories to administer, and their own traditional ways. The Church of Columba and Patrick was monastic in its makeup and was drawn from a different Christian heritage than the Church of Rome, and they were on a collision course. After the fall of the other patriarchs (in Alexandria, Constantinople, and Antioch), the Papacy was left effectively the last man standing, and the Holy See spread its authority across the old Roman Empire in the west.

One by one, local versions of the faith were swept aside—sometimes through conversion, other times at the end of the sword. And one of the key issues in this was Easter.

Like most Christian Holy Days (hence: holiday), Easter was adapted by local churches to fit in with existing festivals: originally in Jerusalem to coincide with the Jewish Passover, and then in northern Europe to replace the old spring feasts associated with rebirth and fertility. Indeed, the word "Easter" comes from an Anglo-Saxon fertility goddess *Ēostre*—hence all the eggs and rabbits. The story of Christ's martyrdom on the Cross, death and resurrection fitted in well with these old rites, and the shift from one to the other was practically seamless. The haphazard adoption, growth, and local methodology of conversion meant that there were lots of different theologies in the early Christian world; and at dispute was the correct way to determine Easter, which had no fixed date like that of Christmas. At its heart lay the thorny problem of reconciling a calculation with the complex celestial clock.

The famous Council of Nicaea in 325AD brought together many various strands of Christian thinking to form a set of rules. Among the rules laid down was the uniformity of the calculation of Easter. Simply put, Easter Sunday will be the first Sunday after the first full moon following the Spring Equinox. This sounds fairly straightforward, if a little pagan, but the reality is far more complicated. The Church uses lunar months rather than calendar months, which can be out of sync by eleven days per year (especially when there is a blue moon—a thirteenth full moon in any given year). The Church determines that the full moon will be the fourteenth day of the lunar month (this may not be an actual full moon). So, using tables, it is possible to determine the lunar month dates and thence calculate the dates in the actual calendar. If this isn't bad enough, there is a bigger astronomical problem: the equinox.

The equinox (literally, "equal night") is the point in the earth's orbit when the tilt of the axis brings the sun directly overhead at the equator, giving everyone on the planet the same length of daylight. However, the earth doesn't quite go around the sun once every three hundred sixty-five days, a problem corrected with leap years, meaning that the spring equinox can fall on either the nineteenth, twentieth, or twenty-first of March. The Roman Church, however, fixed the date in its calendar as the twenty-first. It was the calculation of the equinox that caused the rift between Rome and Iona. The matter came to a head in the English kingdom of Northumbria, a land that was historically faithful to the Celtic rites but had many influencers at court who followed the Roman doctrines and wished to see their local church's practices aligned with Canterbury and York (the principal seats of the emerging church in England) and the Papacy.

So, in 664, King Oswiu convened the Synod of Whitby on the Yorkshire coast to resolve the issue once and for all. The Ionan house still used a very old method of calculating the equinox, while Rome favored more modern techniques. It was a thorny issue—the Pope had decreed that a miscalculation of Easter was a heresy and worthy of excommunication (or worse). The Catholic (universal) Church was determined to bring these remote stragglers on the fringe of Europe into line, and this synod represented something far bigger than the question of Easter. The future Christianity of the British Isles was at stake.

Having listened to both arguments, but faced with political reality, Oswiu came down on the side of Rome. Henceforth, all abbeys and churches across his realm would observe Easter in the Catholic tradition. Although it didn't wipe Iona or her ideology off the map, it was a serious blow that left the small Hebridean community isolated. Other northern kingdoms, such as Pictland, followed suit, and the Ionans were exiled back to Argyll, and once strong daughter houses like Dunkeld were forced to adopt the new calculation. Finally, in 715, with every other religious settlement in line with Rome, Iona accepted the inevitable. It was the beginning of the end for Columba's establishment: Within eighty years the Vikings began their raids, and within one hundred fifty years all authority had been transplanted to the east.

Yet the signs of this old religion are still to be found across the map. Most towns or villages that begin with *Kil* (such as *Kil*marnock, *Kil*malcolm, *Kil*creggan, and *Kil*choman) are derived from the Gaelic word *cill*, meaning "cell," which gives us an insight into the simple, almost hermit-like lifestyle of these Dark Age monks. Most are distributed where Gaelic was most dominant. As the Roman Church was first adopted by the English speakers following Whitby, it stands to reason that this sea change would be reflected in the language—the use of *kirk* (akin to the German *Kirche*) in places such as Falkirk or Laurencekirk became dominant. These churches would be something we'd find more familiar than the austere Celtic monastic cells, but leave us with a legacy nonetheless.

The folk memory of these old saints and their place names lingers, and it is an important part of our etymological landscape. There are several distilleries that still carry on these names, inherited from the original farms, and those names stretch all the way back to the Celtic Church and the men who carried the Word of God around the hills and glens of Scotland. The Christian conversion of a superstitious, but deeply religious people who believed in the "other-world" and their own Gods, fundamentally changed how they orientated their days, weeks, seasons, and indeed view of life itself.

Many farms would also bear the surnames, and sometimes first names, of the families that tilled the soil for generations; others, perhaps, were reflective of the major landlords or noblemen. Whisky making is a byproduct of agriculture, and Scotland is a land long under the plough, and the story of individuals and their names drawn from farming, sweat, and toil into whisky is indicative of the close relationship that the distilleries have with the communities they're centred in and around. Whisky making is local in production, but global in scale—and the men who made it so have left their indelible mark and their famous names.

In the earliest days of the whisky trade, when the good stuff was being smuggled in the dead of a moonless night from the hills to Glasgow or Edinburgh, it was being sold directly to the public houses or went through the tradesman's entrance to the grand houses. There wasn't much in the way of a middle-man (except for the poor souls running the gauntlet by actually moving the goods), and this went for rural areas, too. The whisky was being transported in oak barrels, which they discovered matured the stuff and made it tastier, for the want of a better term, and thus more sellable. So, the industry grew, and new outlets and entrepreneurs got in on the act. There was money to be made at this game now.

Napoleon once described Britain as a nation of shopkeepers; and by his own time, he wouldn't have been far wrong. Until the late eighteenth century people ate and drank what they produced themselves or could barter for at local markets. But as the towns and cities began to grow, and incomes increased with improvements in agricultural output, a new emerging customer base emerged—and with it, provision stores. They were modest groceries to start with, selling farm produce and all manner of drinks, soft and alcoholic. They were also simple apothecaries who stocked lots of weird and whacky remedies and elixirs. In larger stores you could probably get clothes and even furniture and utensils (until this time most people made their own furniture—which, until wood cutting and working improved, meant most Scots had precious little in the way of furniture until the early 1800s). In short, these shops would have resembled the provision stores of the American Wild West, as portrayed in the movies. But soon there would be specialization and diversification of wares; and a nation of shopkeepers was born.

There seems to have been a particular specialization in selling tea, coffee, wine, and spirits together; and I guess that makes a kind of sense. Tea and coffee were new, and while not intoxicating, narcotic. It was eagerly sought after by the intelligentsia of society as well as stores, cafés, and coffee houses popping up in the fashionable parts of town. Wine, of course, had been drunk since time immemorial, but the issue was the spirit. Gin was fiery, and Scotch coarse and cheap—with a very different clientele than the coffee buyers. The merchants started to experiment by mixing the whisky with sugar, honey, and a whole raft of different liquids. Some worked, some didn't—but those that did, sold.

In 1801, the Chivas Brothers opened their provisions store on King Street in Aberdeen, selling a variety of supplies including whisky. Presumably, they bought and sold malt whisky from local producers (possibly even from Speyside—some legal, some maybe not so much), but with the advent of the column still and the production of very cheap grain whisky they must have bought into this as well. Generally speaking, it was the grain whisky that was being mixed with all sorts and sold, as it yielded a higher profit margin.

Essentially, grain whisky is produced as high proof ethanol that is then aged in the cask and watered down. If you like, it's simply aged vodka, but with slightly more flavor (what the vodka industry would call "impurities"). It's made on a massive scale—there's gallons and gallons of the stuff. But it's almost undrinkable by itself, and that was the issue. However, it would be the making of the Scotch industry.

The Chivas Brothers weren't alone. John "Johnnie" Walker invested in a grocery, wine, and spirits merchants outfit in Kilmarnock in 1825, selling first malts, vatted malts, and then from 1830, corrupted grain concoctions; and William Teacher and Sons started selling a "blended malt" whisky in 1832 (a marriage of single malts, known alternatively as a vatted malt). Both of these men would start something they would never have envisaged becoming world famous success stories. But in each case their sons and grandsons would.

This seems to be the case for many of the famous blends we see on the shelf today. Initially, it wasn't legal to create a blend as we understand it (a mix of malt and grain whiskies) until 1860; but when it happened, the floodgates opened, and it was the second and third generations of pioneers who ran grocery stores that grasped the nettle and made Scotch the greatest spirit of them all. Johnnie Walker (the man long dead, but run by his son) created the first of their iconic blends in 1865; William Teacher in 1863. Arthur Bell and his business partner Thomas Sandeman set up a wine merchant business in Perth in 1825, but by the 1840s, Bell was the sole proprietor and was experimenting with malt blending. In the 1860s, he went to London to promote his products. So well received they were that by the 1880s Bell's was only making blended whisky and had become a household name.

David McNicoll

*Figure 4.1 Blair Atholl Distrillery: Heart of the Bell's Blend
(photo reproduced with permission of CPR Photography)*

Jimmy Buchannan, a Canadian born, Ulster-raised Scot, saw the same opportunities in the British capital city. He started out in the grain business with his brother, but then decided to enter the blending game himself, by himself, and saw London as a huge untapped market. He jacked in his other interests and set up a company producing by the 1880s Black and White Blended Scotch. It was a massive success, as was the man himself, who would go on to become first a knight and then a lord of the realm. Closer to home, James Whyte and Charles Mackay set up a merchant's provisions and a bonded warehouse. It didn't take them long to realize that the whisky would make them more money, and in 1882 the blend Whyte & Mackay was born. Matthew Gloag and his grand-nephew, another Matthew, again Perth-based merchants, had been dabbling with blending since the 1860 law change. In 1897, Matthew Junior created a whisky called The Grouse Blend. It became so popular in the local area that it was renamed The Famous Grouse. It remains the biggest selling whisky in Scotland.

In 1879, three bothers, Charles, David, and Gordon Graham, who ran a tea store, chucked their lot in with the increasingly lucrative whisky industry and created a blend called Black Bottle. Originally, the bottle was actually black, but the glass came from Germany, so this came to an abrupt halt in 1914, and it's been green ever since (the use of black glass was actually fairly common, but following the outbreak of war most manufacturers opted for clear glass going forward). The use of the glass, like the shape of the Johnnie Walker bottle or the West Highland Terriers on the Black and White label, has become iconic; but all the imagery and craft in the world is no match for great salesmanship and the gift of the gab; and one whisky above all owes its success to this: Dewar's.

As noted, John Dewar was born in 1805 in a small croft farm nearly one thousand feet above the picturesque Highland town of Aberfeldy in Perthshire. He established a blending business in 1846, very much as others were doing, but it would be the legal changes and the coming on board of his sons, Tommy and Alexander (but called John) that transformed this whisky into one of the most famous in the world. John Junior served as chairman of John Dewar and Sons Ltd. and also went on to become a successful politician, ending up as Lord Forteviot. He was passionate about his whisky, but his brother was fanatical.

As I've previously alluded, Tommy Dewar was one of life's livewires—a raconteur, a comedian, and a visionary.

Jimmy Buchannan and Arthur Bell had, quite rightly, targeted London as an open and ripe market for picking; but Tommy's ambitions were far wider. He wrote a book, *A Ramble Round the Globe*, a series of stories told and collected from his travels promoting his family's whisky. Dewar's was specifically created to cater to a more international palate, and he visited over thirty countries, which at that time was pretty unusual for a businessman. America was where he found a most eager audience, both for his after-dinner speeches and his very easy drinking blend. His vision that Prohibition was nonsense and would end, and his calculated gamble to stockpile whisky for that event, proved to be one of the greatest sales tactics in the industry. Sadly, dying in 1930, he wouldn't see the day when Dewar's White Label would become a mainstay of the American drinks cabinet and its biggest selling spirit.

With the exception of the Chivas Brothers, I've chosen each of these whisky barons not just because of the industry they created, or the blends they bequeathed us, but because despite being owned by multinational companies today (Dewar's by Bacardi, Johnnie Walker by Diageo, Chivas by Pernod, and so on), their signatures still appear on the bottles. A testament to the lasting legacy these fathers of the whisky industry left us—literally, their names liveth forevermore.

PART 2

A NOBLE HERITAGE WRIT IN STONE

"Do not remove the ancient landmark that
your ancestors set up."
—Proverbs 22:28

Scotch whisky is a little bit like the Scots themselves: rooted in history, a strong sense of tradition, and welcome at every party. Over the course of the last decade, the growth in malt whisky sales has been exponential, giving marketing and brand teams around the world a chance to create new and innovative expressions, and to design them in increasingly informative and seductive packaging. Yet one of the key elements to any presentation, whether on the box or by a brand ambassador, is to reach back to the heritage of the brand, to the history. Each tells its own tale and is often reflective of the social history of a particular area.

As we have seen, whisky evolved from an agrarian, self-sufficient, local-market driven world; the locations of the distilleries themselves depended hugely on geography and climate, and to an extent, historical factors. Those locations in turn have unique local stories, varying linguistic heritages, and a myriad of symbiotic (or otherwise) industrial pasts.

Distilleries also only existed in the twentieth century due to their relevance and usefulness to the blenders on the whole, and this was more flavor driven than geographic or historical. So, many pressures have been brought to bear in being successful, but in their names we are looking at over one hundred different reasons and a hundred different stories—some linked to the making of the *uisge beatha*, some with the people who tilled the land, others harking back over fifteen hundred years to ancient priests, and some with the most obscure backgrounds imaginable. And in their names we view a forgotten world far removed from the modern corporations that run the show today, peeling back the layers to reveal the people and places that give whisky their names.

For convenience, I've broken down the whisky producing areas of Scotland into their traditional and industry recognized regions. There were other options such as genre, and taste profiles, but I feel this tells the better, more joined-up story. The social history of whisky and of our distilleries is often overlooked, and we take for granted the labels on the back bar. It is my sincere hope that you find the following both interesting and enjoyable. We begin our journey in that greatest of whisky regions: Speyside.

CHAPTER 5

SPEYSIDE

"Rome was built on Seven Hills—Dufftown on Seven Stills."
                                                    —Local saying

The fast flowing, salmon rich River Spey (*Uisge Spè,* from the Gaelic meaning "gushing river") rushes northeast from the high peaks of the Monadhliath (Grey Hills) Mountains, and through a lush, arable landscape of fields, terraces, and rolling hills stretching toward the snowcapped Cairngorms. At over one hundred miles in length, and with considerable tributaries in the Dulnain and Avon, it drains a decent portion of the north central Highlands, all funneling through the wide vale of Strathspey (*Srath Spè*—"Valley of the Spey"). As it approaches the sea, the land becomes flatter and even more agriculturally rich. This is top barley growing country; and as such, was historically a contested land with lots of internecine warfare and a world decorated with a myriad of castles. The Gordons, the Grants, the Duffs, and other major families would emerge as the principal stakeholders in a wider territory generally referred to as Speyside.

The cataracts raging from spring snowmelt on the mountains around the Spey and her catchment bring cold, clean, fresh water down into this arable corner of Scotland, and it is no coincidence that since time immemorial this has been a whisky making district of the highest order. During the dark days of the malt taxes, there were countless illegal stills concealed amid the many nooks and crannies afforded by the cover of hill and forest; indeed, the very landscape seemed to be designed for the purpose of hiding all manner of equipment, and of course, the contraband itself. It was this very fact, as we've seen, that drove the Duke of Gordon, the principal landowner, to promote the necessary law changes in the 1820s.

Literally hundreds of formally illegal operations came out of the shadows to set up as legit distilleries, and many of them are still with us. However, the majority would, for one reason or another, go to the wall and vanish; the story of the lost distilleries of Speyside is a book in itself. Yet even today, nearly two thirds of all Scotland's single malt distilleries are to be found in this region, a testament to the quality of the water, the abundance of barley, and the legacy of generations of skilled stillmen. And it was to there that the whisky barons, those masters of the blend, came to find the whiskies they needed to build their brands. Whisky's compatibility for blending are graded A, 1, 2, and 3 (although this is an old-fashioned classification and few blenders still use it); all the A graded whiskies are in Speyside. Indeed, there are numerous distilleries that make malt solely for blending and have no named releases of their own, unfamiliar names that form the backbone of the Scotch industry. But there are plenty of well-known names there too, and the biggest of them all is Glenfiddich.

Strathspey was not only an important route north from the mountains to the sea, but also a key crossroads in the world between the Picts and Gaels, and many of the hill, stream, and farm names reflect this, with lots of composites drawn from both linguistic heritages. **Glenfiddich**, globally the largest selling single malt, is such a Gaelic/Pictish marriage and means "The Valley of Fiodhach" and named for a traditional Pictish province, Fidach, the root of which could be a personal name—Fida.

Nearby, and sadly now closed, **Pittyvaich Distillery** also has a Pictish root (Pictish/Gaelic: *Pit à' bhàthaich*—"Farm with a byre"). This may hint at the nature of animal husbandry and communal agriculture in the past, which suggests that not all farmers were employed in cattle rearing. Black Highland cattle, one of the oldest domesticated breeds of all, wasn't just a beef cow; even as late as the nineteenth century they were a form of currency in a cash-poor economy. Indeed, protection money paid by owners to prevent theft was in the old Scots tongue: "black mail" which literally meant payment for black cattle. Thus, a farm with a byre (a cattle shed, rather than a barn, which was a grain store) was probably communally important.

Glenfiddich, which is surprisingly still family owned, sits in the self-styled malt whisky capital of the world: Dufftown. And in addition, today there are five other distilleries here: **Balvenie** (Gaelic: *Baile Bhainidh*—"Bethan's Farm." Bethan was an early Bishop of Mortlach); **Mortlach** (Gaelic: *Mór Ulach*—"Big Hill"); **Dufftown** (English—"Duff's Town"); **Glendullan** (Gaelic—"Valley of the small field by the river"); and **Kininvie** (Gaelic—"The end of the fair plain").

At the time of writing, Kininvie is no longer in operation, but its juice goes into the vatted malt, Monkey Shoulder. Back in the day, when malted barley had to be turned on the floor, each maltman had his own wooden shovel, and by the end of the day his strong arm would droop in a sort of repetive strain injury; and this was called a "monkey shoulder."

Although the actual town of Dufftown wasn't founded until 1817, when James Duff the 4th Earl of Fife had the place commissioned as a planned town to provide work and homes for soldiers returning from the Napoleonic Wars, it was historically however an important crossroads and the seat of the ancient Diocese of Mortlach, created in 1012 by King Malcolm II. The story goes that he defeated a Danish army nearby and, in thanks, enlarged the church and gave it a bishop. The diocese existed until 1132 when its authority was transferred to Aberdeen. In the twelfth century, the Comyn family built a castle there, also originally called Mortlach but later renamed Balvenie after that early bishop. The castle fell first into the hands of the Douglas family and then ultimately into that of the Stewart Earls of Atholl. It was abandoned around 1720.

This corner of the lower Spey—nestled on the main routes leading from the south to the Moray coast (the Moray Firth is a wide inlet of the North Sea), the wild Buchan plateau, and deep into the hills of Strathdon—was a familiar stomping ground for several Dark Age preachers. Saint Moulag, it was said, founded a church there in 566 that would one day become the seat of the diocese, and if place names are anything to go by, he wasn't alone in his evangelizing.

About six miles away from Dufftown, hidden in a grove on a terrace high above the Spey are the ruins and site of a medieval chapel dedicated to Saint Fillan, called *Magh Fhaolan* or "The Plains of Fillan." Time and linguistic moulding has rendered this into English as **Macallan**. Now, there were two Saint Fillans out and about in both Scotland and Ireland during the eighth century, and it is impossible at this distance in time to know which the church of Macallan (the ruins lie close to the distillery) was dedicated to. It is a tenuous stretch that either ever set foot in this part of the country. Option one, the less likely, spent most of his time almost exclusively in Ireland, while the other Saint Fillan roamed central and eastern Scotland finally settlling in Pittenweem on the coast of Fife, north of Edinburgh. Either way, it doesn't really matter—the fame and gravitas of any particular saint would be carried to the four winds by followers, and could, like dandelion seeds, find root anywhere. And legends would be born.

In 2018, Macallan opened a spectacular new production facility on site, and it will be key to meeting demand and propelling the brand forward through the twenty-first century.

This section of the middle Spey is particularly rich in distilleries, including **Craigellachie** (Gaelic: *Creag Eileachaidh*—"Rocky Hill"); **Benrinnes** (Gaelic: *Beinn Ruaidhneis*—"Promentory Hill"); **Aberlour** (Gaelic/Pictish: *Obar Lobhair*—"Mouth of the noisy stream," which is another Gaelic/Pictish composite); **Dailuaine** (Gaelic—"Green meadow"); and **Cardhu** (Gaelic: *Creag Dubh*—"Black Rock"), the heart of the Johnnie Walker blend.

A little further up the road to Elgin lies another little cluster around the village of Rothes, including, among others, **Glen Grant** (named for the two brothers who founded it in 1840, John and James Grant, and upgraded and made famous as a brand by James's son, Major Grant) and **Glenrothes** (Gaelic: *Gleann Ràthais*—"The valley of the circular fort").

Now, it's not my intention to list and give the meanings of each and every Speyside distillery—that would become quite tedious pretty quickly so fecund is the area. But special mention needs to be given to a group that were arranged and named not only by geography but also by opportunistic marketing, and one that would lead to the courts.

The Glenlivets

Today, we're used to bundling the distilleries together into this region or that; this is a relatively modern phenomena; something that gained ground and acceptance following the Second World War. But in days gone by there was one name that stood out, one that was synonymous with quality, a region of sorts with which distillers sought association: Glenlivet. This corner of the Highlands, where the rolling uplands of the rivers Avon (pronounced "ann"), Rinnes, and Fiddich are sheltered by the Cromdale Hills, the windswept peaks of the Lecht, and the foothills of the Cairngorms, was perfect whisky making country and even better for hiding illegal stills. If anywhere could claim to be the heart and soul of the old days of the smugglers, it's surely the Braes of Glenlivet (the term "brae" is a common term in Scotland and simply means slope).

On a visit to Edinburgh in 1822, King George IV strove to be as "Scottish" as possible, parading around in a horrendous travesty of Highland dress, kilt and all, in a piece of theatre choreographed by that master of historical romantic fluff, Sir Walter Scott. And the point of all this pantomime: George was the first monarch to visit Scotland since 1651, and he was keen to build bridges and show off to his Scottish subjects that he was king of all Great Britain. It was a colorful display of tartan fiction that his niece Queen Victoria would come to personify. And while on this jaunt to Edinburgh, His Majesty declared it was time for a whisky—and promptly asked for a dram from Glenlivet.

Many in polite society were aghast that the king had ordered an illicit whisky (after all it was his taxes that were being dodged, and his laws broken). But others saw an opportunity. Following the passing of the Excise Act in 1823, George Smith, a tenant on Gordon's Glenlivet Estate and former illicit distiller, became one of the first people to take advantage by obtaining a licence and building a distillery near the foot of the glen by the water source of Josie's Well. This move did not go down well with his neighbors, still hawking their proscribed spirit and unwilling to make the investment as Smith had. It wasn't just a war of words; on more than one occasion his life was threatened. His friend, George Gordon of Aberlour gifted him a couple of pistols for protection—pistols which were discharged in self-defense and now sit on display in the distillery as a reminder of a less cooperative time.

With the king's endorsement of the name, the quality of product, and the efforts of Edinburgh salesman Andrew

Usher, Smith's Glenlivet was hugely successful. So much so, that in due course "Glenlivets" appeared all over the place—imitation is indeed the best form of flattery. The distillery eventually went to court in 1880 and won an injunction that meant that they and they alone were the definite article—**The Glenlivet** (Gaelic: *Gleann Liobhat*—"The valley of smooth running water").

It was a partial victory however, as the courts allowed the other producers to use Glenlivet as a suffix. Hence, until the 1970s and even into the 1980s we had Macallan-Glenlivet, Dufftown-Glenlivet, Aberlour-Glenlivet, GlenGrant-Glenlivet, and around twenty others that used the term, some of which, such as Tomatin-Glenlivet, weren't even in Speyside at all. It all seems a little ridiculous to us today, but at the time it made perfect marketing sense—the reputation of a Glenlivet-based whisky was that good.

It made sense—unless you were The Glenlivet, of course, who felt that these other distilleries were simply capitalizing on their success; and through various court cases and agreements it was eventually dropped across the board. Macallan even went so far as to become The Macallan, and notions of Macallan-Glenlivet are fading fast, to be found only on rare private bottlings or stenciled on the ends of some of the older casks. In time, of course, Glenlivet came to mean only one distillery, the reputation of the name as a region waned, and was eventually replaced by the rather generic "Speyside."

As well as the Spey, the area's other main watercourse is the River Deveron (Gaelic: *Dubh Èireann*—"Black Earn" as opposed to the "White Earn," which is the River Findhorn. Both may signify ancient Pictish boundaries). The Deveron flows sixty miles from the Ladder Hills to the North Sea at Banff. Again, this is arable hill country, with almost ideal whisky making conditions. From the medieval lordship of Strathbogie, the river flows through the town of Huntly, where the first Gordon lairds made their home and erected a fantastic castle, ruins of which even today are impressive. Nearby, up the Strath is **Ardmore** (Gaelic: *Ard Mòr*—"Large Height"), which produces around a million gallons annually, mainly for the Teachers Highland Cream blend, although there are a couple of age-statement single malt releases. Ardmore is borderline Speyside/Highland, but as the Deveron swings north, it's joined by the River Isla, and the whiskies along its banks are most definitely Speysides.

The principal town on the Isla is Keith, which developed in the Middle Ages around an important crossing of the river on the main route from Inverness to Aberdeen. There are four distilleries there, two owned by Pernod and important malts for their Chivas blend: **Strathisla** (Gaelic: *Srath Ilè*—"Valley of the River Isla." The root of the word "isla" is unknown and probably pre-Celtic) and **Glen Keith** (Gaelic/Pictish: *Gleann Cèith*—"Valley of the Woods;" Cèith is likely to come from a Pictish word similar to Coed). Bacardi has a distillery there for their Dewar's labels: **Aultmore** (Gaelic: *An t-Allt Mòr*—"The big stream"), which in a previous life under United Distillers produced a "Flora & Fauna" range single malt bottling. This continues with whiskies such as

Linkwood, Inchgower and Daluaine. Close by is one that still does produce a F&F label for Diageo: **Strathmill** (Gaelic/English: *Srath Mill*—"Mill in the Valley").

There are a few outliers as well, dotted across the hillsides like sentinels of some long-forgotten kingdom and which ought to get some mention.

The Cathedral City of Elgin sits in a plain known as the Laigh of Moray, a relatively flat land gently sloping toward the sea, and one of the driest and sunniest areas of the British Isles. A medieval kingdom in its own right, the land of Macbeth, Moray is today home to fighter jets and a cluster of distilleries. The name, pronounced "murray," hearkens back to the very arrival of Gaelic as a language in the area, and aptly means the "land by the sea." Close to Elgin, it is retained in the distillery **Glen Moray** (Gaelic: *Gleann Moireabh*—"Valley of the land by the sea"), although in this case there is no actual glen; the prefix is a marketing add-on to make the whisky more sellable (if they couldn't be called Glenlivet, then glen-something might indicate some level of quality), and was common practice.

Founded in 1224, Elgin Cathedral, known as the Lantern of the North, was home to the Bishops of Moray, and in the absence of any real secular power once this semi-independent province was absorbed into the Kingdom of Scotland, these men of God wielded enormous power over a vast territory. This sometimes came back to bite them. Famous is the story of Alexander Stewart, Earl of Buchan leading his wild Highland warriors or caterans into the city and burning the church to the ground. He earned himself the nickname, the Wolf of Badenoch for his rapacious control of the north as the king's son and lieutenant; but this was by far and away his most audacious act.

With such an ecclesiastical presence, it's no wonder that a couple of the local distilleries retain this footprint: **Mannochmore** (Gaelic: *Mannoch Mór*—"Big place of the monks") and **Longmorn** (Gaelic: *Lann Morgan*—"Morgan's Glebe;" a glebe being land attached to a church).

There are a couple other notable distilleries in the area, such as Linkwood (English, as is) and Benromach near Forres. **Benromach** comes from the Gaelic and means the "shaggy mountain" (*Beinn Ròmach*); the hill itself lying a few miles south of the town and from where the spring water comes. Today, it's owned by Elgin-based private bottlers Gordon and Macphail, who release it in various single malt expressions. The peated version is unexpected for the region and one of the author's go-to's. Forres is also home to **Dallas Dhu** (Gaelic: *Dalais Dubh*—"Black Water Valley"), which since 1992 has been a museum preserving past methods and machinery, and is in the hands of Historic Scotland. It's well worth a visit if you're in the area, as is the Cooperage near Dufftown, if you're interested in seeing how the casks are made.

Back up into the mountains are two final distilleries to mention (among a myriad of others that I apologize for ignoring): **Glenfarclas** (Gaelic: *Gleann feur glas*—"Valley of the green grass"), which is one of the very few independents left in Speyside, and **Tomintoul** (Gaelic: *Tom an t-Sabhail*—the "Hill of the Barn"), which along with Dalwhinnie is one the highest distilleries in the country. So, there from its commanding position on the hills above Glen Livet, Tomintoul looks down upon the greatest whisky-producing country on earth. Bounded to the east by the Deveron, and to the west by the Findhorn, Speyside is the true inheritor of the Pictish past. Moving on, we head to the heart of the Gaeldom: The Islands.

CHAPTER 6

THE ISLANDS

*"From the lone sheiling of the Misty Island, mountains divide
us and the wastes of seas; but, the blood is strong and the
heart is Highland, and we in dreams behold the Hebrides."*

—Canadian boat song

The beautiful Isle of Islay is home to another grouping of distilleries. Nine in production at the time of writing, with more likely to come online in the next few years, it is a malt-lovers' paradise. The island lies at the southern end of the Hebridean archipelago, a chain stretching along the west coast of Scotland, of which around fifty are inhabited. The origin of the name Hebrides is unknown and is likely to be pre-Celtic. They were first described by the Roman writer Pliny the Elder around 50 AD as the "Hebudes." Today, they are collectively known in Gaelic as *Innse Gall*, or the "Islands of the Foreigners;" a reference to a near four hundred-year-long Norse colonization, from the eighth to thirteenth centuries.

Similarly, Islay as a name has an unknown origin and again is likely to be pre-Celtic (there are a few others with equally obscure roots: Mull, Skye, Tiree, and Rùm). Pliny called Islay

"Epidion" which may be related to a peoples known by the Romans at the time as Epidii, or "The Horse Tribe," which occupied nearby Kintyre and Mid Argyll. Interestingly, the clan name MacEacharn, which comes from the same area, translates as "Sons of the Horse Lord." The MacEacharns certainly lived on Islay long before MacDonald, and laterally, Campbell rule of the island.

Saint Adomnàn of Iona, writing in the seventh century, referred to the island as "Ilea," and from the end of the Norse period, which would be around 1150, the spellings included: Yla, Ila, and the modern Gaelic name, *Ìle*. The spelling Islay (pronounced "eye-la") is the English equivalent. Whimsically, it is often referred to by locals as Banrìgh Innse Gall, meaning "Queen of the Hebrides."

Although rightly famous for her whiskies, Islay also has a rich heritage and wonderful scenery. So, if you ever plan a visit, make sure to include gems such as the Kildalton Cross (perhaps the best example of a carved Celtic cross in the British Isles); the Mull of Oa (a fantastic cliff walk with spectacular views over to Ireland); Machir Bay (a beautiful beach out in the west); and Finlaggan (seat of the mighty MacDonalds, the Lords of the Isles who ruled the Hebrides between the twelfth and fifteenth centuries). There is also a rich Gaelic heritage and a wonderfully relaxed atmosphere to the place. And of course, there are the distilleries. Let's start with the oldest.

Bowmore (Gaelic: *Bogh Mòr*—the "Big Reef") was founded back in 1779 in what was then a newly designed town by the same name. Daniel Campbell built the place in 1770 based on a grid pattern sloping down the hill from the round parish church. The church is rounded to stop the Devil from hiding in the corners. It was said that the locals chased the Devil out of the church, and he ran down the hill to the distillery and hid in one of the casks, and that this was sent unknowingly to the mainland (the brand, owned today by Beam-Suntory, has capitalized on the myth with their expression "Devil's Cask"). Bowmore is the largest town on Islay and sits near the head of Loch Indaal, a long fjord that gives the island a sort of horseshoe shape.

On the opposite shore lies **Bruichladdich** (Gaelic: *Brudhach a' Chladdich*—the "Stony Slope"); a distillery founded in 1881 and then resurrected a little over a decade ago. It sits below a raised beach, a remnant of an ancient coastline formed at the end of the last ice age. As ice sheets across the world began melting around 13,500 years ago, sea levels rose dramatically—much higher than today—and indeed, for a while Islay was two islands. The land itself had been depressed into the crust by thousands of feet of ice, and it, too, rebounded, but over a longer period of time. The result today is a land still rising and old beaches left high and dry, sometimes far from modern coasts. Those old Islay beaches were rockier than the present soft-sanded beaches around the island. Thus, the "Stony Slope" is an apt description. As a geography major I digress, so back to the subject in hand: Bruichladdich also produces expressions called Port Charlotte (the nearby town named for Charlotte Campbell) and Octomore, a farm that means "Big Eighth Farm" and where this expression sources its barley.

That side of the island, known as The Rhinns (Gaelic for "promontory") is also home to the recently established

Kilchoman Distillery as well (Gaelic: *Cill Chomain*—"Saint Comman's Church"). This is the only distillery on the island that is not at sea level, which indicates the changes in transportation. Earlier distilleries relied on boats, while today, road haulage is the preferred option. Saint Comman lived in the second half of the seventh century, and his brother was the Abbot of Iona. It is likely that he was preaching in an area already converted to Christianity, and his church would have served the local population. There are numerous saintly references on Islay, probably due to the proximity of the island to Ireland and Iona; indeed, Saint Columba is said to have first made landfall on Islay before settling on Iona. (The ancient meaning for Iona probably means "Island of the Yew Tree," which would have symbolic meaning for Celtic druids, but today is rendered in Gaelic as *I Chaluim Chille*—"Iona of Saint Columba." The sacred yew tree tradition may have been his reason for establishing the monastery and community there in the first place).

In the south sit another three well recognized malts: **Lagavuilin** (Gaelic: *Lag a' Mhuillin*—"Mill in the Hollow." Milling is an essential part of the whisky making process, so historically it made sense to have them close to each other, if not cheek by jowl); **Laphroaig** (Gaelic: *Lag a' mhor aig*—"Hollow by the big bay"); and **Ardbeg** (Gaelic—"Little Height"). These sit close to Islay's other main town, Port Ellen, which until 1983 had a working distillery of its own: **Port Ellen** (English—"Port of Elinor," named after Fredrick Campbell's wife). Today, all that remains are the Diageo Barley Maltings and the original skeltall buildings. Promisingly, the company has indicated that the distillery may once again rise from the ashes and go back into production, which would be exciting to see.

Figure 6.1 Laphroaig Distillery and Palm

The last distilleries are on the north and east side of the island: **Bunnahabhain** (Gaelic—"Mouth of the River") and *Caol Ila* (Gaelic—"The Sound of Islay," a sound being a narrow sea channel). In 2018, a new distillery opened between these two established sites: **Ardnahoe** (Gaelic/Norse: *Àird na Hogh*—"Promontory of the Burial Mound").

Scotland is one of the most amazing places on earth. In a land of superlatives, the Island of Islay holds a special place for me personally: from long sandy beaches, friendly faces, great whisky and a tent that I thought would be blown all the way to Ireland. Just ask my wife.

Across the sound, a mere three thousand feet away, is the wild Isle of Jura, a rough, mountainous land stretching like a spear back toward the Scottish mainland and dominated by the Paps (the "Breasts of Jura"). At one hundred forty-two square miles, Jura is more than six times the size of New York's Manhattan Island, but while Manhattan has a resident population of over 1.6 million, Jura is home to one hundred ninety-six hardy souls. There is only one road on the island—the road—and most of the population is centred on the one village, Craighouse. And it is there we find the distillery **Isle of Jura** (Gaelic: *Eilean Diùra*; from the Norse: Dýrøy—Island of Deer").

This is an island with mystery and legend in every corner—from the enigmatic Sgriob na Caillich (a line of boulders that stretch down the hillside on the western side of Jura, meaning literally "The Writing of the Witch") to the Gulf of Corryvreckan, or Coire Bhreacain, meaning "Speckled Cauldron," the third largest whirlpool on earth. Even the distillery has some spooky goings on: it was said that the founder was inspired by a ghost, and their Prophecy expression is based on a true story of Second Sight. Superstition and myth haunt the Highlands and Islands to this day as we've seen, but on lonely Jura there really is sense of the Otherworld.

The town of Tobermory on the Isle of Mull, famed for its row of brightly colored houses, was, like Bowmore, a planned village, built on a natural harbor in 1788 by the British Fisheries Society on a scheme again designed by Thomas Telford. The distillery, founded by John Sinclair in 1798, was originally called **Ledaig** (Norse: *Lad Aig*—"The pile or heap on the small bay"). Indeed, it is only relatively recently that the name of the whisky produced on site was changed to **Tobermory** (Gaelic: *Tobar Moire*—"Mary's Well"), although they continue to produce an expression called Ledaig. The well provides the distillery with its water source, and is named in honor of the Virgin Mary, harking back to a time when the islands were predominantly Catholic in worship.

The long influence of the Viking Norse reaches deep into the history and culture of the Hebrides, and as we've seen with Jura and Ledaig, lent their tongue to the very names of these whiskies. Another is the world famous Talisker on the Isle of Skye. Lying in the shadow of the mighty Cuillin Mountains, **Talisker** (Norse: *t-hallr Skjaer*—the "Sloping Rock," and rendered into Gaelic as *Talasgair*) was, until recently, the only distillery on what is probably the most beautiful, and certainly most dramatic of the Scottish islands. The Gaelic name for Skye is *An t-Eilean Sgitheanach* which is of uncertain origin, but possibly means "The Winged Island." The English name is less doubtful: coming from the Norse, "*Skuy*" which translates as "Misty Isle." (*Eilean a' Cheò,* meaning the same in Gaelic is a familiar and informal name for the island).

Skye is the second largest of the Hebrides and has a population of just over ten thousand. This has been a fairly stable number over the last twenty years or so, but considerably lower than the unsustainable twenty-three thousand in 1841 that eaked out a living ahead of the depressing and brutal Clearances that would follow. On a cheerier note, it's dominated by its almost Tolkienesque landscape—from the Black and Red Cuillin mountains in the south, through Macleod's Tables in the west, to the Fairy Glen, the bizarre Cuithraing Hill formations, and the breathtaking ridge of the Trotternish in the north.

This is a land of superlatives. It was also a land bitterly contested between the Clan Donald and the Clan Macleod for centuries, with several battles and plenty of murders along the way. The Chief of the Macleods lives at Dunvegan Castle, and it is the longest continually inhabited castle in Scotland—nine hundred years. It is said that the chiefs are descended from the fairy people, and that the Fairy Flag of Dunvegan (a scrap of material held in the castle) will protect them in battle. Talisker, the village, lay around five miles from the distillery, and was historically all Macleod land. However, in 1825, it was sold to Hugh MacAskill (who founded the distillery five years later). Sadly, he would go on to evict many tenants during his ownership leaving even today a fairly lonely (albeit beautiful) corner of the land.

It's not all bad news. Following the Napier Royal Commission into the Clearances in the 1890s and the laws it would bring, a brutal landlordship could (theoretically) no longer haunt the people of the Highlands. The story of the Seven Men of Moidart in the 1950s was the last act in a stubborn horror show of oppression. Clouds were parting. Like a phoenix, even the Gaelic language would see green shoots, and Skye was on the front line.

Starting in the late 1960s, there began a resurgence in promoting, developing, and above all, teaching the Gaelic language. Today, there are numerous Gaelic-medium schools across the country. One of the biggest advocates of this, and the pioneer of the dual-language road signs found on Highland roads, was Sir Iain Noble, who in 1973 established a Gaelic College on the Sleat (*Slèite*—"Level Field") peninsular at Sabhal Mòr Ostaig (the Big Barn). It has been a phenomenal success, from humble beginnings. A few years back, the Mossburn Distillers started to work on development of a distillery on the estate, and the result was the first fully operating distillery on Skye since the establishment of Talisker. From 2017, this new facility, **Tòrabhaig** (Gaelic/Norse: as written, probably—"Peat Bay," or a reference to a personal name) began producing its single malt. These farm-style distilleries are part of the future success of Scotch and critical for the economies of small communities in the Highlands and Islands.

Skye, as an island and a people, is a truly amazing place. A visit shows you why so many legends and stories come from there; but much more, they've preserved and promoted their unique cultural identity in a fast-changing world (which differs from that of Mull or Islay or Lewis, which are all equally unique). So, as the cloud rolls off the high, black, and foreboding peaks of the Cuillin, take a moment to sit back, take a deep breath, and enjoy a dram or two on this misty and enduringly special isle.

Across the narrow sound from Skye lies the quiet and sparsely populated island of Raasay; where in 2017, a new distillery was opened and will start selling its first single malts in 2020. This distillery, as we've seen elsewhere in the Hebrides will play an important part in supporting a small, fragile communitiy. The name comes from the island itself: **Raasay** (Gaelic: *Ratharsair*—"Island of the Roe Deer"). It is a detour, but worth it. From the extinct volcanic peak of Dun Caan, to the incredible endeavours of Callum MacLeod and the road he built with his own bear hands over twenty years to link the north and south of his island, hopefully the new distillery will breathe life into this wonderful place.

Three other west coast islands also have distilleries: **Arran** (probably Old Welsh: *Aran*—"High Place") is on the hilly island of the same name, in the wide estuary of the River Clyde, downriver from Glasgow. **Lagg** (Gaelic: *An Lag*—"The Hollow"), run by the same team as Arran, is situated at the southern end of the island and hit production in 2017; and their visitor center opened in June of 2019. The whisky produced is a full bodied peated number.

Abhainn Dearg (Gaelic—"Red River") on Lewis in the Western Isles; and the nearby, newly established **Harris Distillery** (probably Norse: *Hérað*—a "land portion" in the Viking western tongue). Like north Raasay, Lewis and Harris are underpinned by some of the oldest bedrock on earth, and certainly the oldest rock in Europe—the 3.8 billion year old Lewisian Gneiss. Terroir doesn't really affect whisky making, but it's thought provoking to think of the source water flowing to two of Scotland's newest distilleries is coursing over rocks lain down when life itself was first emerging.

Speaking of the Norse, there are a couple of northern outposts on the historically rich Orkney Mainland that cannot go unmentioned.

The Orkney Islands lie off the far north coast of Scotland and are home to two distilleries. The oldest (1798), and the most northerly distillery of them all, is **Highland Park** (English—"High Park"); and the other down the hill by the coast, a half mile away is **Scapa** (Norse: *Skalp*—"Boat"). Both look out over the wide harbor of Scapa Flow, one of the world's largest and most sheltered bays, and home to the Royal Navy Fleet during the First and Second World Wars. And it wasn't just twentieth century warships that saw the value in the Flow; this was a key base for the Viking expansion of the whole of the northern Atlantic. By the twelfth century, the great Earldom of Orkney extended power all the way to Dublin, subordinate only in theory to the King of Norway. Indeed, not until as late as 1472 did the Scottish Crown gain control of these incredible islands from the Northmen.

The distilleries are in the main center of Kirkwall (Norse: *Kirkvoe*—"Church Bay") which is aptly named for the huge Saint Magnus Cathedral that towers over the narrow street-lined town. It's an attractive corner of the world: a fishing village surrounded on three sides by flat rolling hills, and it is the hills to the south that are historically the High Park, or High Farmland, as well as from where the distillery gets its peat and name. However, despite the Viking (and later Scottish) heritage, the story of the Orkneys goes back millennia in a way unlike anywhere else in Britain. Even the magical Stonehenge pales.

Figure 6.2 Saint Magnus Cathedral, Kirkwall

111

Both the Orkney Mainland and the myriad of outlying islands in the archepelagio have impressive prehistoric remains. Chief among them are the Standing Stones of Stenness, the Ring of Brodgar Stone Circle, Skara Brae Prehistoric Village, and the truly incredible Maeshowe burial chamber. All these date back over five thousand years to the world of the first farmers in the north of Scotland. Collectively, the Heart of Neolithic Orkney is a World Heritage site, and nowhere in northern Europe has such a concentrated collection of sites been preserved. The Orkneys are agriculturally fertile, albeit virtually treeless, reminicent more of rural Aberdeenshire than the Highlands, and surrounded by abundant seas fecund in haddock, cod, and shellfish. It was also an important staging post during the hey-day of the whaling industry. During the Iron Age its agricultural output would have made it a relatively rich part of the country, and with that it probably had a highly organized social structure.

Around 300 BC, Pytheas of Massila, a Greek explorer, described Great Britain as being triangle-shaped, and at the northern tip, he called the area "Orcas." The Romans called the Islands "Orcades," meaning "Young Boar" (apparently, the "King of Orkney" was one of the eleven British leaders who submitted to the Emperor Claudius in AD 43 at Colchester—a sign perhaps of the wealth and influence of the local chief). In the old Irish Gaelic, the islands became rendered as *Innse Orc*, and then into modern Gaelic as *Arcaibh*. When the Vikings arrived, they reinterpreted the name as meaning "Seal Islands" or *Orkneyjar*, which was shortened to Orkney.

112

The Norse influence is everywhere, not just in place names, but in the very fabric of society, the dialect, and in buildings all over. The Earls of Orkney were powerful princes, but by the fifteenth century they were being drawn from Scottish families rather than Norwegian. The Scottish legacy is just as compelling, and the evidence of a continued history in places from the Broch of Bursay to the winding flagstone streets of Stromness; or more recently the Italian Chapel and Churchill Barriers from the Second World War. It shows a place not only rooted in the distant past but very relevant today and with an international reach. It is thus fitting that people from across the globe visit this compelling jewel of a place—a land where the ancient meets the modern, and yet where time stands still.

The Scottish Islands each have their own stories, their own individual character and landscapes, people and social history—no two are alike. The whiskies reflect this and are ever evolving, from the eighteenth century distilleries at Bowmore or Tobermory to the newly established at Kilchoman, Raasay, and Abhainn Dearg. There are new possibilities, too, on Islay and Harris, and maybe even Shetland. There are currently twenty distilleries in operation across the Islands, some producing smoky whiskies, others light and fragrant; it's a genuinely eclectic range. But believe me—no whisky tastes better than at sunset overlooking the azure sea as the last ferry leaves, and solitude and peace returns.

CHAPTER 7

THE LOWLANDS

"It was the best of times, it was the worst of times."
—Charles Dickens

Around 350 million years ago, the land that would one day become Scotland lay far to the south of its present position, straddling the equator, with a hot humid climate (slightly different than today). A high range of mountains that would one day become the Highlands swept down to a wide plain that had over the course of the previous twenty-five million years been sporadically dry land or under the waters of a shallow sea. At the edges of this sea and up briny estuaries was a great swamp forest, a tropical paradise (that included, amongst other things, a giant sea scorpion) with trees as far as the eye could see. This was a sharp contrast to the mighty inland desert beyond the hills.

This period, known as the Carboniferous, began with a stretching of the crust to create the rift valley that would eventually evolve into Scotland's Central Belt, a land of volcanoes belching out ash and fire; the remnants of this more violent time we can still see today in famous landmarks like Edinburgh and Stirling Castle rocks. Massive rivers on the scale of the Ganges or Yangtze flowed out of the mountains and laid huge amounts of sediment on the floor of the plain, which in time would solidify into the Old Red Sandstone that underlies much of the Lowlands.

With every encroachment of the sea, limestones and chalks would be laid down underpinning the bedrock of vast tracts of east and southern England including the famous White Cliffs of Dover. At the end of this balmy period these swamps became the graveyard of truly mind-boggling amounts of dead forest material, which would solidify, carbonize and ultimately under massive pressure form into coal. Meanwhile, far out to sea, dying marine creatures were slowly forming the pockets of hydrocarbons that would fuel the Scottish oil and gas industry.

The legacy of this incredibly verdant and abundant time would power the world's first Industrial Revolution, which in turn would shape the look, nature, and personality of the Scottish Lowlands and her people. However, it is a legacy that we have to temper considering Climate Change today. With implications political, economic, and cultural, we in our ancient land must still fully realize this is a Devil's bargain indeed!

Water is key in whisky making—good, clean, fresh, cold water—and the geology through which that water flows has an impact. Kentucky bourbons, for example, are made where water flows through limestone to remove unwanted iron. Though, this is not a problem across most of Scotland. As mentioned, geology, or the terroir, doesn't have the impact that it does on the wine or beer industry. However, there are nuances imparted that can be carried into the spirit and even into the matured whisky. The Lowlands may have a very different geology to the Highlands and Islands, but there are plenty other factors at play that make each of the whiskies in the region different not only from the others, but from each other as well.

Coal and iron found in massive deposits around the Central Belt provided the raw materials upon which a powerful industrial base could be built in the eighteenth and nineteenth centuries; and Glasgow (Gaelic: *Glaschu*— "Green Hollow") was the greatest city of them all, becoming known as the "Engine Room of the British Empire." Here, sitting on the River Clyde was a town that had begun life as a monastic community before morphing into a trading port; and capitalizing on its access to the sea with a commercial heritage, it took full advantage of a myriad of resources. Iron forging, steelworks, manufacturing, pottery, and of course, shipbuilding. By 1900, two out of every three ships sailing the world's oceans was built on the Clyde; and those ships took all the produce that Glasgow and her hinterland were making and sold it around the globe.

It all came at a human cost, of course. This industrial leap forward required man-power, plenty of it, quickly and on a consistent conveyor-belt. Not until the middle of the twentieth century did birth rates overtake death rates in British cities, so migration was paramount. Immigrants flooded places like Manchester, Sheffield, Liverpool, and of course, London. In Glasgow's case, they came from Ireland (over 13 percent of all inhabitants by 1900) and the Scottish Highlands, and the population mushroomed. In 1800, the population of the city was around eighty thousand. By 1900, it has risen to nearly eight hundred thousand—a ten-fold increase within a hundred years. The economic and political implications were enormous. Beyond London, the world had never witnessed anything like it.

For the city's tycoons, it was a boom time, and the splendid architecture of George Square, the Merchant City, and Blythswood are testament to the money-making. There was another side to Glasgow though: people tended to live within a short walking distance of their jobs, which meant that they were crammed in, cheek-by-jowl in nearby tenements. By the 1840s, the squalor and sheer deprivation in places like Cowcaddens or the infamous Gorbals was horrific. Perhaps up to one hundred thousand people per square mile, sharing sometimes fourteen to a room in run down houses with little or no sanitation. There was no welfare state or National Health Service there, and life expectancy was appallingly low. When cholera hit in 1849, 3,777 people died; and then another 3,885 in 1854 (this would be against a background of other ever-present killers like polio and TB). Something had to be done—and the answer would be part of the story of Glasgow's distilleries.

In 1855, the City of Glasgow Corporation Water Department began work on an ambitious project to bring the clean, fresh water of the Highlands down to the city. Loch Katrine, a lake about forty miles north of Glasgow in an area known as the Trossachs, was artificially raised, and thirty-nine miles of aqueducts and tunnels would supply water under head of pressure without pumping to the masses. It was a superlative feat of civil engineering, and Queen Victoria herself opened the system in 1859. When cholera hit the city again a few years later, you could count the dead in double digits, rather than in the thousands. It is hard for us in our buy-a-bottle-of-clean-water world to comprehend how monumental that was. Today, up to fifty million gallons can be delivered daily; but not all of it destined for the city's inhabitants.

Not necessarily all producing at the same time, there have been at least twenty distilleries at one point or another in Glasgow—even one amid the bleakness of the Gorbals until 1823. Two of them drew upon the main supply once it came in from Loch Katrine, and with the huge success of the public water supply works, any association with something so clean in such a grimy town would have positive connotation: and consequently be marketable. Thus, Camlachie Distillery became "Whitevale Loch Katrine" and Adelphi, "Adelphi Loch Katrine." Seven distilleries made it into the twentieth century, including the two above, and one—Kinclaith— would see its malt facilities dismantled as recently as 1975, the building absorbed into a greater grain distillery.

At the time of writing, there are only two single malt distilleries in production in Scotland's largest city: **Auchentoshan** and the brand new **Clydeside**, opened for operation in 2017. It's named for the River Clyde itself, (Gaelic: *Abhainn Chluaidh*, derived from the older Brythonic name, Clut. Known to the Romans as Clota, the name meaning is obscure, as are many river names in Scotland. It is possibly pre-Celtic and perhaps in honor of a water goddess). It is a product of the region's resurrection, and at least two other distilleries are on Glasgow's current radar.

Auchentoshan (Gaelic: *Achadh an t'oisean*—"Corner of the field") is technically not in the city, but in Dalmuir, which is part of Clydebank; although, in reality, it all rolls into the sprawling two million people conurbation that is Greater Glasgow. Until 1870 the area was rural with a number of farms and larger estates stretching from the river to the Kilpatrick Hills, and Auchentoshan appears on maps as a farm going back into the eighteenth century, and as an estate in the records going back to 1516 when it belonged to Paisley Abbey.

After the Reformation, the land, it seems, was split. The farm that would become the site today was owned firstly by the Johnstone and then Buchanan families, who lived in a mansion house on the estate (little remains today, and most of the land is now a golf course). Buchanan sold the farm to John Bulloch in 1817, who then founded a distillery. It proved a false start, and not until 1823 did things really get going, and this is the date you'll find on the bottles today. However, intriguingly, the name might be suggestive of a time when covert distillations had to be concealed from the authorities. Did some old-time, rudimentary still get hidden in the corner of the field?

In 1870, with industry expanding and the ships being built ever bigger (and thus needing deeper water), Glasgow, for all intents and purposes, swamped the small villages around Dalmuir. In that year the population of Clydebank was around fifteen hundred; within thirty years that number had swollen to over thirty thousand. Shipyards dominated the landscape, but there were other new industries as well—the largest Singer Sewing machine factory in the world was built there. And while living conditions weren't great, they were better than in the city. As an aside, Singer was based out of Harrison, New Jersey and about a thirty-minute train ride from New York, if the gods of public transport were on your side. But the expertise was honed in Clydebank, and managers and technicians were sent over the pond. As a result, even today many street names are Scottish and there are pipers, ex-pats, and even a haggis shop in nearby Kearny.

Sadly however, the name Clydebank is ingrained in the Scottish psyche due to the events of the 13th and 14th of March 1941, when it was repeatedly bombed during a two-night blitz by the German Luftwaffe. The glow from the fires (including exploding barrels at Auchentoshan) could be seen from the hills of Aberdeenshire two hundred miles away. Hundreds were killed and thousands made homeless. But Glaswegians, like most Britons, are resilient, and while it took time, they bounced back. Until recently, the brochure for visiting the distillery told you to leave the A82, turn right at the cemetery, and left at the crematorium—because clearly, people were dying for a shot. Graveyard humor is never far from Glasgow's soul; and maybe at times, that is just what is needed.

Throughout this rapidly changing world one thing has remained constant: Auchentoshan has always triple distilled its spirit, all 100 percent of it, and this makes it unique, as today it is the only Scotch that fully does this. Until 1993, **Rosebank** (English, as written) also made a triple distilled single malt. It may have been a Lowland feature, perhaps a hangover from a time when higher proofs were required in the gin making process. For Auchentoshan, it might be more to do with Irish migration into the Glasgow area (seasonal agricultural laborers), and Irish whiskey is traditionally triple distilled. The higher ABV (alcohol by volume) that results from three distillations (around 81 percent) when combined with the barrel wood makes for a different beast. Looking forward, if the proposed **Falkirk** (Old English: *Fa' Kirk*—"Speckled Church") distillery ever gets off the ground it also plans to produce a triple distilled spirit.

To bring the story full circle, the water for Auchentoshan and Clydeside does not come locally, but all the way from Loch Katrine; an endurance of good quality water meeting good quality whisky making. Glasgow's whisky legacy continues to benefit from a genial solution to a Victorian social problem. I predict the city's whisky revival is only just beginning.

Scotland's industrial complex stretched right across the Lowlands, with each town and city specializing in a particular trade depending on its geography, local resources, proximity to market, and traditions. Dundee wove jute, Falkirk made nails and pitch, Alloa had brewing, and Fife, Ayrshire, and Mid Lothian had coal mining.

The Scottish capital, Edinburgh (Gaelic: *Dùn Èideann*— the "Fort on the Slope"), however, developed slightly differently, due to its function as the seat of the administration, politics, and law. Banking, scientific research, education, and publishing were at the heart of this most academic and financially driven of cities. The so-called "Athens of the North" did have more manual professions, too—principally, printing and brewing. And amid these temples of money and legislation there were distilleries as well.

Most of Edinburgh's malt distilleries were located in the north around the Port of Leith (Gaelic: *Lite*—"Wet" or "Damp"), which would make sense, as this is where most of the grain would come in. Also, the land in the eighteenth and nineteenth centuries between Leith and Edinburgh proper was still arable and the water reasonably uncontaminated. As the two towns converged, the availability of land and the rising value of real estate would have made production difficult. Only two made it into the twentieth century: **Dean** (Brythonic: *Dene*—"Deep Valley") which was closed in 1922 and **Glen Sciennes** (French: *Sienne*—the old local monastery's association with the mother house in Italy). Like many others it was abandoned in 1920s.

However, Edinburgh does still have a working distillery—a grain distillery, **North British** in the Gorgie (Brythonic: possibly *Gor Gyn*—"Upper Wedge") area of town. This is a vast production, making around fourteen million gallons of spirit a year (compare Macallan at around two million). Most of the grain used is maize imported from France (through Leith, as in days gone by). The spirit produced can either be used to make Smirinoff Vodka, or provide the grain whisky bases for Johnnie Walker, Famous Grouse, and Cutty Sark blends (the enterprise is a collaboration between the Edrington Group and Diageo). Following the Treaty of Union in 1707, there was an attempt by the London establishment to officially rename Scotland as "North Britain." It never quite caught on but is retained in a few commercial interests still out there.

To the west of Edinburgh, shale oil mining was a major industry prior to the discovery of North Sea oil, and to the south, the city is skirted by large coal fields, now mostly exhausted with all the mines closed. To the east, where the soil is rich, the land flat, and the climate warm and dry, is some of the most arable land in Scotland. And there, near the village of Pencaitland, about fifteen miles from Edinburgh's city center, is **Glenkinchie Distillery** (Gaelic/ French—"Valley of the De Quincey family").

As we saw when I discussed the Anglo-Norman influence of David I and the adoption of the Feudal system into Scotland in the twelfth century, the king brought minor nobility and knights north to help activate and implement the new order. The De Quincey family came originally from Cuinchy in northern France (near Calais), but by the time David was living in England, they had established themselves in Northamptonshire to the north of London. Saer De Quincey was married to David's stepdaughter, and thus, the connection that brought him north. They seem to have had land and influence in Fife, but as the name suggests, in East Lothian around Pencaitland, too. It also seems that they lost their lands when they supported the English king, Edward I against Robert the Bruce during the Wars of Independence in the early fourteenth century.

The name lives on though in the Kinchie Burn, the small stream upon which the distillery was built in 1825, originally called **Milton Distillery** (English—"Mill Town"). The burn runs off the Lammermuir Hills, and rather unusually for a Scotch through limestone rock. This means the water is hard (as opposed to the soft waters of the Highlands), which imparts unique characteristics on the whisky. The hard water helps control the pH, and the minerals stamp certain flavor profiles during fermentation. The whisky is very light, grassy with a bit of citrus, and even slight ginger notes. The distinctive geology has surely a role to play in this.

There are a few other single Lowland malt distilleries, most of which, like Tòrabhaig on Skye, are brand new. A couple of examples from this part of the country are **Daftmill** (literally in English, the "Daft Mill") and **Lindores Abbey** (possibly Brythonic—"Church by the pool") in Fife (Gaelic: *Fiobh*—an ancient name, maybe personal). Yet, Fife, for all its fame for fishing, corn, and coal, was once home to a raft of distilleries, from **Invekeithing** (Gaelic/Pictish: *Inbhir Cèitein*—"mouth of the wooded stream") to **Cupar** (Gaelic: *Cùbar*—"common land") a bewildering thought as you cross this enigmatic county today.

Another new distillery that began operating in the hills between Fife and the plains of Lowland Perthshire in 2017 is **Aberargie** (Gaelic: *Obar Fhargaigh*—"Confluence of the wrathful stream") near the fair city of Perth. In the Waverley Novels, Sir Walter Scott recalls a fanciful, although possible event when the Romans crossed the hills at this point and saw the estuary of the River Tay from this spot. According to legend, the weary legionary looked down upon the Tay and uttered the phrase: "It's the Tiber." In Scott's words: "Behold the Tiber!" the vain Roman cried, viewing the ample Tay from Baiglie's side; But where's the Scot would the vaunt repay, and hail the puny Tiber and call her the Tay?" One hundred fifty miles away from the silvery Tay is one of Lowland Scotland's true survival stories.

The southern-most distillery in Scotland is **Bladnoch** (Gaelic: possibly *Bladach Cnoc*—"Small hill by the wide mouth"), near Wigtown close to Stranraer, where you catch the ferry to Belfast. The Gaelic origin of the name tells us a little bit about this area and its heritage. Galloway derives its modern name from Gall-Gaidel, which is an older Gaelic form that means "Foreign Gaels," which like the Hebridean Innse Gall, points to an established Gaelic-Norse rule in the area around one thousand years ago (the modern Gaelic is Gall-Ghàidhealaibh, which means the same). The distillery has opened and closed more often than a grocery store, and with multiple owners, but is thankfully still part of the story.

The Norse-Gaels established kingdoms all along the west coast of Scotland, the Isle of Man, Cumbria, in what is now England, and an enclave around Dublin. The medieval rulers of Galloway were Gaelic-speaking descendants of the men who colonized these areas and married into the local community. Galloway was absorbed into Scotland in 1235 by King Alexander II following the death of the last Lord, Alan of Galloway. The language persisted in remote pockets in this hilly country, with the last recorded speaker of local Gaelic dying as late as the 1730s. The place names of the area reflect a heritage that originally began as the Welsh-speaking kingdom of Rheged, then the Norse-Gaels, and finally English. Bladnoch is a fine example of the lost tongues of old.

So, three fully fledged distilleries survive, with thankfully more firing up, such as the **Borders Distillery** in Hawick (Old Scots: *Havwic*—probably, "Village surrounded by a hedge"), located in the Southern Uplands, close, as the name would suggest, to the border with England—the first distillery in the Borders in over one hundred eighty years; and **Holyrood Park** in Edinburgh (Old Scots: *Holy Rude*—the "Holy Cross") next to the Queen's official residence in Scotland, the Palace of Holyroodhouse, and due to come online in 2019.

These are a scattered fragment of a time when nearly every town in southern Scotland had their bakery, brewhouse, and distillery. Some were short-lived enterprises, and some made it into the twentieth century, only to be killed by Lloyd George's taxes, the Depression, or consolidation of the big boys. Some, however, lasted a lot longer and may still be found in dusty cupboards in specialist shops (and online of course). These include **St. Magdalene**, Linlithgow (closed 1983); **North Port**, Brechin (1983); **Glenflager**, Airdrie (1985); **Littlemill**, Bowling (1985); **Glenury Royal**, Stonehaven (1986); **Lochside**, Montose (1992); and **Rosebank** (1993).

However, as you wistfully look back teary-eyed on paradise lost, it's not all doom and gloom. Like Dracula from the grave, a phoenix is rising. In 2018 Ian MacLeod Distillers, a private enterprise which includes Glengoyne in their portfolio, have vowed to bring Rosebank back to life and the local authorities have given them the green light. As an old name with a new vision, it will surely be an important page in the next chapter of Lowland, triple distilled whisky.

Blended whisky makes up nearly 90 percent of total global Scotch sales, and as noted, blends are essentially grain whiskies flavored with a selection of single malts. These distilleries, like North British in Edinburgh, are massive operations, and the majority are in the Lowlands. The names will be unfamiliar, and it is highly unlikely that you will see a bottled version on the shelf (there are some out there though); but given that nine out of every ten Scotches sold around the world are blended, it is very likely you have drunk these whiskies in one guise or another; thus, they deserve a mention.

Cameron Bridge (Gaelic/Pictish (possibly)—"Bridge by the crooked hill") is a single grain that you can find in some select outlets (mainly, at Diageo visitor centers) and is the largest and probably best known of all the grain distilleries. Originally built by the Haig Whisky family in 1824, it was one of the first to employ the column still (the type invented by Robert Stein), and by the end of the twentieth century under Diageo ownership it was producing around thirty million gallons annually. In 1989, it was also converted to produce grain neutral spirit, which meant its output could be turned into vodka or gin. Tanqueray, Gordon's Gin, and Smirnoff Vodka are produced there, as well as the whisky that goes into Johnny Walker, Bell's, Haig, and other blended brands.

The Cameron Bridge, which the distillery is named after, crosses the River Leven at one of the lowest crossing points during flood times; and nearby are Cameron House and the Cameron Cottages.

Other working grains in the Lowlands include: **Strathclyde** (Old Welsh: *Ystrad Clud*—"Valley of the Clyde"), **Girvan** (Gaelic: *Gearr Abhainn*—"Short River"), **Loch Lomond** (Gaelic: *Loch Laomainn*—the "Beacon Loch." The loch is named after Ben Lomond, the Beacon Hill). Loch Lomond also produces single malt. And the newest additions are from the Glen Turner company: **Starlaw** (Gaelic/Old English (possibly): *Sturr Hlāw*—"Rough Hill") in Livingston; and one from the Mossburn stable in the Borders, called **Reivers Grain** (Old English: *Rēafian*—"to rob." The Border Reivers were notorious bandits and mercenaries that crisscrossed the border as a sort of mafia-cum-private militia from the thirteenth to seventeenth centuries).

There is one other grain distillery—**Invergordon**—that lies in the Highlands. The town, essentially a planned village, was named for Sir William Gordon, a local landlord and long-time member of Parliament. It was long known that large vessels could berth safely in the deep waters there where the Cromarty Firth meets the North Sea; this allowed for ships to dock and provide the distillery, set up in 1959, and operational from 1961, with grain (large cruise ships also regularly berth at the town, and its deep waters have served the oil industry for decades). The distillery is owned by Whyte & Mackay as their provider for grain whisky, which in turn is owned by United Breweries, a large but troubled Indian corporation. Diageo is now the major stakeholder, and the future is very uncertain.

Invergordon is not the only distillery in Easter Ross, the fertile lands north of Inverness on the A9 trunk road corridor; the abundance of the barley crop there would see to that, and as a whole, they are part of the wider Highland Region.

CHAPTER 8

THE HIGHLANDS

"Oh, Chi mi na mòr bheanna."
"I will see the great mountains."
—Traditional Gaelic Song

It's common currency to believe that malt whisky can be pigeon-holed into regions like wine, based on character, flavor profiles, and so on; and perhaps on Islay this could be true, and to a lesser extent in Speyside, with some underlying similarities. But, with so many new distilleries joining the pantheon and seemingly never-ending line-extensions even this is becoming tenuous at best. The Lowlands have such a dearth of distilleries, and those that do exist express such different production methods and geologies that really each is a region unto itself. But it is with the Highlands, in my opinion, that the notion of an overarching regionality genuinely falls down.

There are nearly three hundred miles of wild country separating the southernmost Highland distillery with the northernmost; some are coastal, while others lie over one thousand feet above sea level; some have big rounded stills producing robust, oily malts, while others, slender stills and long lyne arms, giving us more delicate and light whiskies. The choice of casks and length of maturation vary, and the geology underwrites the water source. So in all, it's a bit of a mixed bag. However, look a bit closer and you will see that many of the distilleries are clustered, almost mini-regions, and this is probably the best way to break down this large whisky group.

The Northern Highlands

The Northwest Highlands, apart from a few coastal towns and villages is one of the last truly remote and isolated corners of the British Isles. Here is a near-treeless landscape, a patchwork of heather moorland and rocky mountain interspersed with shimmering lochs and the occasional green valley snaking towards the sea. It is spellbinding and an area of genuine outstanding natural beauty. From these high hills, fast flowing rivers like the Conon and the Oykel foam toward the east coast and the three, deeply indented estuaries of the Dornoch, Cromarty, and Beauly Firths, and their lush and verdant hinterland.

Figure 8.1 Suilven from Inbhir Pollaidh Forest

This is flat, rolling, arable country resting on sandstones and other sedimentary rocks laid down in some long-lost prehistoric lake; it provides a stark contrast to the wild mountain land only a few miles to the west. And the climate, too, is chalk and cheese. The town of Ullapool on the west coast receives around sixty inches of rain a year, while Inverness on the east coast gets a mere twenty-six inches. It all adds up to another one of those key areas where cold water from the hills meets rich barley growing land in the vale.

This agricultural haven forms a sort of "Fertile Crescent" from the Laigh of Moray around Inverness, through Easter Ross and the Black Isle, to the slopes of coastal Sutherland around Golspie. It is in this narrow region that nearly 75 percent of the Highland population is to be found. It is also home to seven single malt distilleries and one grain (the already mentioned Invergordon).

At the heart of this productive region are the domains of Easter Ross (Gaelic: *Ros an Ear*—"Eastern Promontory") and the Black Isle (Gaelic: *An t-Eilean Dubh*), both with long histories stretching back through the mists of time. Battles between Vikings and the Scots, or between warring clans, have been fought there; even 'witches' and seers have been burned alive on its rocky shores. Kings, chiefs, and holy men have all laid claim to this patchwork of hills and fertile meadowland. Amid the whirl of the modern world there is still a detached feel to the quiet towns and villages that dot this corner of Scotland.

For the majority of the last thousand years, much of these lands—as well as a vast tract leading over the moors and mountains to the west coast and beyond, to the Isle of

Lewis—was the world of the Clan Mackenzie. Their huge territory was punctuated here and there by clan holdings of the Rosses, Frasers and the Munros, but for the most part it was the Sons of Kenneth, whose chief (currently the Earl of Cromartie) is known as Caberfeidh which means the "Stag's Antlers," who ran the show. And these antlers tell an interesting tale, one that would be woven into the story of **Dalmore** single malt (Gaelic: *Dail Mór*—the "Big Meadow").

The story goes that the king Alexander III (1241–1286) was out hunting in the great Forest of Ross some seven hundred fifty years ago when he fell from his horse (this would become something of a habit for him, and it didn't end well) and was about to be gored to death by a huge white stag with an imperial crown of antlers. One of his retainers, the chief of the Mackenzies, sprinted to his monarch's rescue and killed the aforementioned stag, thus saving the king's life. So grateful was Alexander that he granted him lands on the Black Isle, around the Cromarty Firth, and west in Kintail, centered on Eilean Donan Castle. As origin legends go, it's pretty fanciful stuff, but the imagery is huge.

The story itself may be a corruption of the stag attempting to maul an earlier king, David I, in the forests of Edinburgh, but who was saved by divine intervention (a cross appeared behind the stag). And in giving thanks, David established a monastery on the site. Perhaps the two tales somehow got woven together. Either way, the antlers are to be found on both the crest of the Mackenzies, and Dalmore distillery, which sits on traditional clan lands, and retains the antlers on their bottles and packaging. They even have an expression known as the "King Alexander III" in recognition of the story. The motto of the clan is the Latin, *Luceo non uro*, which means, "I shine not burn;" which would be very apt for any decent whisky, and unsurprisingly has been adopted by the Dalmore brand itself.

As an aside, the man who founded Dalmore in 1839, Sir Alexander Matheson, was the nephew and business partner of Sir James Matheson, and both men made their vast fortunes selling Indian opiates to the Chinese illegally. Opium was the scourge of the Chinese Empire, and it would bring it to its knees. To protect the trade, Britain acquired Hong Kong, where the Mathesons and fellow Scots, the Jardines, would set up one of the biggest mercantile enterprises in the east. With his money, Sir James bought the Isle of Lewis from the dowager Countess Seaforth, wife of the last earl; the old chiefly branch of the Mackenzies. Despite being a drug baron, Sir James was teetotaler and never drank. Once he acquired Lewis, he made it very clear that he would tolerate no distilleries on his land. This is the reason the island has had a dearth of whisky making, until the advent of Abhainn Dearg. Curious how interconnected these things are.

Across the Alness River is **Teaninich Distillery** (Gaelic: *Taigh an Aonaich*—"House at the meeting place"), which was founded by Hugh Munro in 1817. The flat meadowland here at the crossing point of the River Alness sits where the road from the south forks with that heading west over the Struie Hill to the Kyles of Sutherland and beyond. Another fork strikes to Tain, Dornoch and the far north. It would indeed have been an excellent meeting place. In addition, the lush grasslands around the river would have been especially important for cattle drovers, and from whom the name probably derived as the vast herds converged. The use of 'House' is in my opinion a euphemism for a tavern. A read of Robert Burns' "Tam o' Shanter" will bring you up to speed.

Figure 8.2 Dornoch Firth

At the northern end of the Easter Ross peninsula is the town of Tain. Long associated with Saint Duthac, a ninth century priest (in Gaelic, *Tain is Baile Dhubhtaich*, or "Duthac's town") who may have been born there. It was considered an important sanctuary and a place of pilgrimage; and certainly, there was a very early church built there. Pilgrimage sites always attract lots of people, and where there are people, there is trade; and in 1066, King Malcolm III gave the town Royal Burgh status, the oldest in Scotland, with special market privileges. It also sits in arable country with good access to the sea, so it is no surprise that there is a distillery there, too—and a familiar name at that.

Glenmorangie (Gaelic, possibly: *Gleann mór innse*—the "Vale of the big meadow by the water") was founded in 1843 by William Matheson on the site of an older brewery dating back to the 1730s (there is a long tradition of brewing in the area); and today, it is the biggest selling single malt in Scotland. An elegant and light dram, thanks to having the tallest stills in the game. For over ninety years it was owned by the Macdonald family from Leith (Macdonald and Muir Ltd), but in 2004 it was sold as a subsidiary of the French giants Moët Hennessey-Louis Vuitton.

The name is often mispronounced, and the emphasis should always be on the second syllable—GlenMORangie. The adding of "glen" as a prefix was, as we have seen in other cases, probably done to make the whisky sound more appealing, more romantic and nostalgic, and thus, more sellable (as we saw before with Glen Moray). On older maps from the 1820s, the farm is simply called "Morangie," and the stream is recorded on even earlier maps as the Morangie Burn. So, it is unlikely there was a "Glenmorangie" as such until the distillery was built.

A few miles further along the coast, close to where the modern A9 highway crosses the Dornoch Firth, is **Balblair Distillery** (Gaelic: *Baile Blàr*—"Settlement on the plain"). Founded in 1790, it is one of the oldest in the Highlands. Now owned by Inver House, which in turn is part of International Beverage. Thai Beverages is the parent company and consequently Balblair is a big player in the Far East market. The plain that the distillery is located on is known in Gaelic as *Eadar Dun*, which means "Between the Forts," reflecting ancient Iron Age struggles for control of this vital land. The area is littered with standing stones, stone circles, and prehistoric settlements. This was clearly a key location in days gone by, and by the tenth century a new invader was eyeing its precious dark soils.

The origin of the name "Tain" is a little obscure, but it may come from the Norse word "thing," meaning place of assembly or parliament (the present day parliament of Iceland is the Althing; of the Isle of Man, Tynwald; and of Norway, the Stortinget—all of which have this root). At the head of the Cromarty Firth lies the town of Dingwall, which also takes its name from "thing," and recently, the site of the assembly was found under a carpark of all places.

Although later than in the Islands, this forward expansion of Norse power on the mainland came in 1015 with Thorfinn the Mighty, and it comes to represent the southernmost reach of the Viking realms in the north. Their hold on Easter Ross was fleeting, and soon the Scots had pushed the northern invaders back across the Dornoch Firth (Firth of Tayn in early maps; the Scottish term firth comes from the Norse *fjǫrðr*, "an inlet of the sea," and cognitive with Fjord in Scandinavia), where they would consolidate their holdings in the land of the Cat People.

The Countess of Sutherland (who is ninety-eight at the time of writing) is known to her people in Gaelic as Ban Cataibh Mór, or the Great Lady of Sutherland. Cataibh is an old term, which generally equated to the eastern district of this large county. Cat, or Cait, was one of the ancient realms of the Picts as recognized by Roman geographers covering the far north of Scotland. The name is retained in Caithness (Cape of the Cat; the "ness" element is Norse in origin) and the old Gaelic name for Shetland, *Innse Cait* ("Isle of the Cat"). Shetland itself is Norse for "island shaped like a sword hilt." It is believed by scholars that the name is exceedingly old and may hearken back to a very early Celtic tribe that held the Wildcat (or possibly the lynx, which didn't become extinct in Scotland until around 700 AD) as their totem.

To the Norwegian Vikings who first took control of Shetland and Orkney as bases by which to extend control around the coast to the Irish Sea, and even on the Scottish mainland, this was the *Suðrland* or Southern Land, and from where the modern name is derived. Norse control continued until 1375, when authority passed decisively into Scottish hands. From then, a slew of Earls of Sutherland (and Earls of Caithness) as well as powerful Bishops sitting in Dornoch Cathedral, held sway over this vast, yet sparsely populated northern land.

Those who did live in the interior, in places like Strathnaver or Strath Kildonan, were systematically removed from their homes during the brutal Highland Clearances at the instigation of the Countess Sutherland and her grim agents, or factors. Sutherland is a byword for the Clearances, and the worst excesses came in the early nineteenth century when factors such as Patrick Sellar and James Loch forcibly removed thousands from the valleys. Many emigrated; but those who chose to stay on the Sutherland Estate (which by that point was around a million acres) were replanted along the shore, where after generations of being farmers, they had to learn to become fishermen. The only exception was along the east coast, where there is a narrow strip of fertile, arable land stretching from the Dornoch sands to the flat lands of Caithness. Here farming was 'permitted'—it would add profitability to the estate: very compassionate.

The countess married a wealthy English lord, the Marquess of Stafford, George Leveson-Gower. In 1833, the king elevated the pair to the Duke and Duchess of Sutherland. Leveson-Gower was at the heart of much of the clearing and resettling, and in some small part of his mind he felt he was genuinely improving the lives of his tenants. One of his initiatives was, in 1819, to build a distillery amid the fertile east to provide a ready market for the locally grown barley. No doubt the rents reflected this. The distillery was set up in the coastal town of Brora, and called **Clynelish** (Gaelic: *Claon Lios*—"Sloping Garden"). The "garden" in question refers to the south and east facing, productive soils of Clynelish Township and the sloped terraces behind the town.

As was usual for distillers in the boom and bust Victorian Age, Clynelish had some hairy moments in its history, and finally having survived the downturn—the First World War and Lloyd George's taxes—it was saved from closure by being bought by DCL (Distillers Company Ltd., formed in 1877 by the merger of six whisky producers) in 1925, the same year the company merged with Johnnie Walker and John Dewar and Sons. DCL was bought by Guinness in 1986 in one of the dodgiest deals in the drinks industry and renamed United Distillers. Eventually, UD would become part of the Diageo empire when Guinness merged with Grand Metropolitan.

In 1967, DCL opened a new distillery on the same site, which they called Clynelish, and closed down the old production. However, it was brought back to life in 1969 to produce a peated malt to go into various blends, substituting for the Islay malts, which were on low production due to a drought. The company renamed the old distillery **Brora** (Gaelic: *Brùra*, from the Norse—"River with a bridge"), and it remained in production next to new Clynelish until 1983 when it again closed. Old stock is still available but getting rare and pricier every year. Diageo have committed themselves to a revamp and will probably fire up the stills once more. The bridge over the River Brora is as important today as it must have been to the Norse rulers who found it noteworthy enough to make special mention of it; and it still carries the A9 north to Thurso and Scrabster Bay, where you can catch the ferry over to Orkney: a brief window into the realm of the Vikings.

So, these five, along with **Old Pultney** in Wick (George Pultney was a popular local member of Parliament), **Royal Brackla** (Gaelic: *Breac*—"Speckled") in Cawdor, east of Inverness, and **Glen Ord** (Gaelic: *Gleann an t-Òrd*—"Valley of the rounded hill") in the village of Muir of Ord, a little to the west of Inverness, make up the clustering of distilleries in the far north; but there were others. The city of Inverness (*Inbhir Nis*—"mouth of the River Ness") used to boast three working single malt distilleries: **Glen Albyn** and **Glen Mhor** (both names are versions of the Great Glen which runs between Inverness and Fort William, and includes the famous Loch Ness) both shut down by DCL in 1986, and **Millburn** (English—"Mill Stream") by the same group in 1988. Caithness also used to boast a distillery in Thurso— **Ben Morven** (Gaelic: *A' mhor bheinn* – The big hill) and

Gerston (possibly Norse: *Geirr ston* – Spear Pole) in the village of Hawkirk.

While distilleries in the north have closed, the green shoots are evident with the opening in 2015 of **Glen Wyvis** in the town of Dingwall on the Black Isle (Gaelic: *Gleann Uais*—"Glen of Terror" or possibly, "Glen of the Spectre"). The name derives from the remote vastness of neighboring Ben Wyvis, a huge mountain plateau, where it is said that the Clan Munro hold their lands by virtue of furnishing the queen on demand with a snowball on a midsummer's day—the snow rarely completely melts on any given year on the high tops.

Additionally, and more recently, two more have come into production: **Dornoch** (Gaelic: *Dòrnach*—"Pebbly Place") on the north side of the estuary of the same name. The cathedral city of Dornoch has a dark secret: it was the site of the last witch execution in Scotland, in 1727. Also, in more recent times it was there that Madonna married Guy Ritchie in the old church. The other new build lies on the southern side of the estuary on the Tarbert peninsula of Cromarty near Tain: **Toulvaddie** (Gaelic: *Toll a'mhadaich*—"Lair of the fox," or possibly, wolf). Opened in 2018, it is the only entirely woman-owned distillery in Scotland at the time of writing.

The Northeast

Aberdeen (Gaelic: *Obar Dheathain* – the mouth of the river Don) sits on the North Sea coast, where the cold gray waters mirror the immovable silver rock that the town was hewn from, and locally known as the Granite City. Historically, Aberdeen was an important market town, seat of a bishop, and reliant on a burgeoning fishing industry. A university was established by King James IV in 1495, third oldest in Scotland, devolping as a top center for education, it became a beacon of the enlightenment and agricultural revolution. More recently, with the discovery of oil offshore, Aberdeen has become a wealthy commercial hub for the surrounding community. Yet it remains stubbournly rural at heart; still the old fishing-cum-market-cum-university town commanding the life of its large and varied hinterland.

Aberdeenshire lies north of the Highland line, but thanks to the nature of the underlying geology most of its eastern half is fairly level, non-hilly, plateau land; while to the west through Straths Dee and Don, the land becomes increasingly mountainous, rising over 4,000 feet to the lofty peaks of the Cairngorms. Eighteen thousand years ago, huge glaciers ground their way east toward a wide tundra plain that now houses the North Sea. They gouged and grated the bedrock from the hills into a mineral-rich till or debris that was laid down across the northeast as the ice's momentum waned, and the glaciers melted back into the high ground; eventually vanishing altogether.

In time, that debris would develop into a highly nutrient soil, albeit a rocky and stony one with a wide range of angular boulders strewn across the countryside as the ice retreated. It would be a tough landscape to tame and bring under the plough. Three hundred years ago, most of the heartland of rural Aberdeenshire was a patchwork of rough cattle grazings, heather moorland, peat bog, and a myriad of marshes and lochans. Although, there were green oases of fertile, grain-growing land scattered around—an indication of the quality of soil underneath, an agricultural goldmine waiting to be tapped.

By the end of the eighteenth century, a lot of the land remained uncultivated, and there was still a good, local supply of peat for domestic fuel. The problem of availability would arise over the ensuing fifty years as more and more land was brought under the plough and more coal had to be brought in by necessity. There were few trees, although new plantations had been planned around Meldrum House, and most of the arable land was still laid out in strips known as the runrig system. By 1845, all this had changed. The principal crops grown were oats and barley, but turnips and potatoes were fast becoming staples; this, in turn, helped the growing cattle industry.

Although the Aberdeen-Angus breed we all know and love didn't come into being until the 1840s, it was raised from an older breed stock known as Angus Doddies, and those cows would have been raised on the increasingly rich and pastured fields. Oats and turnips were instrumental crops in improving beef yields. Enclosure, which again happened around 1800 in the north, also helped increase and dramatically advance the productivity of the farm by reducing cattle disease and indeed theft. There was also a radical new form of plough that yielded more for less work. That and other new farm technologies, along with a shift in husbandry and crop choices, was at the heart of an agricultural revolution and it transformed the stony ground of the northeast into a rose garden.

As the potential was being realized, there was a growth in population as well as productivity, and new markets for meal, barley, beer and of course whisky grew exponentially.

The River Don, which like the Spey flows from the snow-capped plateau of the Cairngorms, meanders through the heart of the old medieval county of the Garioch, a world anchored firmly in rural Aberdeenshire. From the Gaelic, *Garbh Iochd*, Garioch (pronounced "Geerie") translates as "rough howes or heathland" and shows us a snapshot of the land there before the agricultural revolution; a world before a time when all those stones were gathered up to make the never-ending miles of walls and dykes crisscrossing the hills. The two principal markets in the Garioch are Inverurie and Old Meldrum; and in the latter, in 1797, the Manson family, taking full advantage in the rise in barley production opened **Glen Garioch Distillery**, which still runs strong under the Beam-Suntory family of brands.

The Mansons came from both a merchant and a farming background and saw the opportunity, literally, in the shifting landscape around them. Within a generation, the whole economy would be changed, and it was important to be part of it. In some sense, Glen Garioch was both a recipient of that transformation, but also very much part of the zeitgeist that was doing the transforming. They also saw beyond their own rural world; it would be a member of the family that twigged that malaria was passed by mosquitos; an understanding that changed the world of disease forever.

Between the previously mentioned River Deveron and the headwaters of the picturesque Ythan River lies a narrow, but gentle, defile: **Glendronach** (Gaelic: *Gleann Dearcnag—*

145

"Valley of the Brambles," or blackberries). Brambles, being a mainstay of the traditional autumn harvest, need relatively dry conditions and proximity to good, clean running water to thrive. That water, less abundant than in other parts of Scotland, would be turned to making whisky. The distillery there, bordering on a Speyside, but most definitely Highland, was opened in 1826 by James Allardice following the lifting on many of the restrictions and the changes to the tax laws. The agricultural improvements across the region saw many new ventures pop up; but sadly, most failed within a few decades. Them's the breaks.

Water, or the relative lack of it (annual rainfall locally is twenty-two inches), was an issue that dogged the northeast. Indeed, Glen Garioch's future was in some doubt until Mr. Stanley Morrison (of Morrison-Bowmore) bizarrely brought in a diviner to find an additional water source. If you believe in such nonsense, you'll believe anything. However, there's a kernal of truth to it: your man with the sticks found an untapped underground water souce and the distillery was saved. As he lived out his days pulling rabbits from hats he was eternally proud of this. Fluke is the word that comes to mind.

Those that did survive from those early days were few and far between. **Benachie** (Gaelic: *Beinn na Cìche*—"Hill of the Breasts"), near Inverurie, would exist from 1822 to 1915, succumbing to forces beyond the scope of a water diviner. **Glenugie** (Gaelic—"Valley of the River Ugie"), near Europe's largest white fish port. Peterhead, was founded in 1821 on the site of a defunct windmill and came a cropper in 1983 amongst the turmoil of whisky's economic downturn.

Glenglassaugh (Gaelic/English: (possibly) *Gleann Glas haugh*—the "Valley of the fallow meadow") takes its name from its water source, like many distilleries; although this translation may be flawed and the root much older, back to a language we'll never reconstruct and beyond the scope of this book. Reconstruction however is the name of the game at this far-flung whisky outpost. Glenglassaugh, too, was mothballed in the 1980s, with old stock going toward the Edrington Group's blends, such as Famous Grouse and Cutty Sark. However, it reopened in 2008 (production starting again in 2009) by the Scaent Group. The BenRiach Company, which also owns Glendronach, bought the distillery in 2013, and the future looks bright. In a way, Glenglassaugh's story is that of Scotch over the last thirty years: doldrums in the 1980s with mass closures, only to come back Lazurus-like in the 2000s with the latest boom.

That boom, like elsewhere, has also seen the establishment of a distillery within the Deeside Brewery that should be online and running sooner rather than later.

Highland Perthshire

The Highland Boundary Fault cuts the great county of Perth in half—from Aberfoyle in the southwest, to the ski slopes of Glenshee in the northeast—and this mighty division creates a land of contrast. The southern half is fertile farming country with rolling acres of rich, dark soils. In areas like Strathmore and the sweeping Carse of Gowrie, the land is so productive that it can support much more than just barley or potatoes; indeed, green vegetables, oilseed rape, and most famously, soft fruit such as raspberries and strawberries (this is among the best berry growing country in the world). That said, there is a history of whisky making amid the berries, with two distilleries having made it into the twentieth century only to be closed like others: **Isla** (Gaelic: *Abhainn Ìle*—a pre-Celtic river name) in Perth and **Stronachie** (Gaelic: possibly, *An t-sròn a ciche*—"Small hill of breasts") in the Ochil Hills near the town of Kinross. Stonachie still exists as a name at least as a private expression owned by AD Rattray and sourced from the Benrinnes distillery in Speyside.

The Highland district is dominated by the large basin of the River Tay, Scotland's longest river and the one with the largest capacity volume of any river in the British Isles. Abound with legend, we have already seen it stealing the affection of many a Roman soldier. The Tay itself has its source on the beautiful alpine slopes of Beinn Laoigh and runs through the heart of the district, collecting tributaries along the way, each of which flow from the farthest reaches of the county. Along every strath and glen the land is relatively fertile with barley or potatoes; but as the altitude increases, this gives way to cattle grazing and ultimately to sheep farming, deer forest and grouse moorland. There are several peaks in excess of 3,500 feet, with the 3,984 feet Ben Lawers the highest of them all, and some wild and bleak country in between, including the smoldering wilderness of Rannoch Moor and Forest of Atholl. It is a beautiful place, with large tracts of ancient woodland, breathtaking views, and a long and celebrated history. It has been a magnet for tourists for centuries.

Like Strathspey and Easter Ross, this district also has the right combination of mountain water, arable land

and proximity to market to have made whisky making commercially viable.

There have been at least thirty-five distilleries in operation at one time or another in Highland Perthshire; and probably many more, as only those who applied for licenses are recorded. Principally, they were clustered around Pitlochry, Aberfeldy, and Dunkeld, which makes sense, as those are the main population centers. They are also well connected by road and rail (Aberfeldy was on a branch line until 1965, and the distillery there even had its own siding) to Perth, and the markets of the Central Belt. Yet, while geography is crucial to distillery distribution, as we've seen in the case of Sir James Matheson, so is a benevolent landlord.

For most of the last five hundred years this part of the world was owned by three people: the Earl of Breadalbane, with a massive half-million acre estate stretching from the central Highlands to the Atlantic coast; the Duke of Atholl, whose three hundred thousand acre landholding covered the north and east of the country; and the Menzies family, whose estates stretched from their castle in the lush Strath of Appin to the windswept wastes of Rannoch. These were powerful men, with authority over every individual living and working on their land. Today, the Breadalbanes are long gone, finally succumbing to the financial meltdown of the 1920s and an inconvenient lack of male heirs. The chiefdom of Clan Menzies would go down the same rabbit hole and were virtually obliterated in 1910.

The Atholls faired a little better but were forced to sell off large areas to cover death duties and keep the bank at bay. They would be bailed out by the wealthy Pearson family, who married into the ducal family. And when they, like their neighbors the Campbells of Breadalbane, ran out of heirs, their estates passed from the traditional owners, the Murrays, into that of the Campbell-Prestons. The estate continues and thrives (Bruce Murray, the current twelfth Duke of Atholl may not own the castle or estate, but he retains the right to raise his own private regiment: the Atholl Highlanders). Breadalbane was shattered into a thousand pieces.

John Murray, the fourth Duke of Atholl certainly had no problem with distilleries on his lands; and in the early to mid-nineteenth century there appeared a slew of small-scale farm-cooperative distilleries. They were set up to provide whisky for local consumers and travelers on the Great North Road, which had just been upgraded by Thomas Telford. There were regular inns on this and other key routes, and they all had to be furnished with the good stuff.

The railway didn't arrive into Dunkeld at the southern end of Atholl until 1856, and not to Pitlochry and Blair Atholl until 1863. When it did, it revolutionized the economies and tourist potential of these picturesque Highland towns. But before the trains started arriving, local hostelries, hotels, and no doubt the great lairds in the castles and "big hooses" had to rely on a regular but local supply for their dram. The farming cooperatives were in a good place to meet that demand, and of course, they made a profit; that, in turn, meant cash rents for the duke. No wonder he was all for it.

There were several inheritors of a thriving illicit industry in the district, of which a few endured into the twentieth century: the tiny **Grandtully** (Gaelic: *Gar an Tulaich*—"Den at the green hill"), which, unable to withstand the tax changes shut up shop in 1910; **Auchnagie** (Gaelic, possibly: *Achadh na Gaoithe*—"Field of the Winds"), which closed under the ownership of John Dewar and Sons in 1912; and **Ballechin** (Gaelic: *Baile Eachain*—"Settlement of the Horse"). As a name this would be resurrected recently as an expression by a fourth, and still active, "farm" distillery built in the area: **Edradour** (Gaelic: *Eadar dhà Dhobhar*—"between two waters").

Figure 8.3 Edradour Distillery
(photo reproduced with permission of CPR Photography)

The two waters in question are the Edradour Burn (which considering the etymology, suggests that it was named after the estate through which it flows) and the Aldour Burn. That estate is centred on Edradour House, which lies on a raised terrace between the streams. Compact estates, and associated ferm-touns (the cottages and community that existed back when farming was labor intensive), usually had a flour mill; several old maps clearly show this one, called Milton of Edradour. And there the farmers set up a distillery in 1825. This is one of the few distilleries that retains an on-site bottling facility and is arguably the most charming of them all.

The Burn of the Aldour (*Allt Dobhar Chù*—"burn of the otter"), also known as the Kinnaird Burn (*Ceann Àrd*—head of the higher land") rushes downhill, cutting through the gravels and clays deposited in long-lost lakes that once skirted immense glaciers and now form long terraces running along the valleyside. As it reaches the valley floor, it slows, and the waters are drawn off to make the **Blair Athol** single malt (Gaelic: *Blàr Athall*—"Plains of the northern routes"). Relatively unknown outside Perthshire, or circles of aficionados, Blair Athol is the soul of the Bell's Blend, and a great sherry casked malt in its own right. These streams have their source on Ben Vrackie (*Beinn Bhreac*—"Speckled Hill") and run over various strata of hard metamorphic rock and some granite outcrops. This makes the water perfectly soft for whisky making. A note of interest is the churchyard nextdoor, where the grave of Sir Robert Watson-Watt, the Scotsman who invented radar during the Second World War, rests.

Streams and rivers are obviously vital to whisky making, and while people tend to think of Scotland as a rainy country, a month or so without any significant precipitation can cause some serious production issues. To our ancestors, a reliable source of water was crucial, and thus revered. In pre-Christian days, many of our Celtic Gods dwelt in watery places. Offerings of valuable and sentimental value were often thrown into lakes and rivers to appease them; this is the likely origin of the Lady of the Lake and Excalibur's magical rise from the waters for Arthur. **Aberfeldy Distillery** has its etymological roots in such a myth (Pictish/Gaelic: *Obar Pheallaidh*—"The confluence of the stream of Peallaidh").

Until relatively recent times the people of Scotland, particularly in the Highlands, believed in legions of mythological creatures and entities that lived in the shadows between our world and theirs. And with this came all sorts of superstitions, legends, stories, and rituals. Some of them have lingered to our times, but to our ancestors these things were real: mostly harmless, sometimes mischievous, and some darker elements that were downright malevolent. The sidhe, or the fairy people, were the most well-known and to be treated with caution, as they had all sorts of magic that could be wielded. Anthropologists tell us that this belief in the sidhe could be an ingrained folk memory going back into the Neolithic, and that horizon shift that came with iron and the Celtic culture. Perhaps some, those connected to the great stone circles, took a little longer to convert, having hid in remote areas and when riled, called upon old knowledge and practice.

Whatever the origin, these superstitions were certainly the inheritance of ancient traditions that existed in the days before Christianity, Columba, and the Cross. And they never really went away and became a sort of sub-religion in the remote mountains where Church influence was minimal amid a life that was hard, marginal, and governed by nature and all manner of things unknown. I'm not entirely sure we've shaken this altogether.

One such ethereal being was known as an Ùruisg (rendered "Urisk" in English). A sort of hermit-like water sprite, the Ùruisg lived in streams, especially near waterfalls, and at certain times of the year would emerge to engage in things like harvests or sowing, and would be paid in kind by the people. The linguist William J. Watson said that it was believed that every stream in the land of Breadalbane was occupied by an Ùruisg, and that their king was Peallaidh. It is understood that he lived under the spectacular Moness Falls above Aberfeldy; and thus, this king of the water sprites gave his name to the town, and of course, to its whisky.

Perthshire's other two active distilleries technically lie to the south of the geological Highland Line but are considered to be Highland malts on the whisky map. **Glenturret** (Gaelic: *Gleann Turraid*—"Valley of the dry river" or possibly, "Valley of the graves") is Scotland's oldest distillery, founded in 1775, and is another in the "farm" style of Edradour, and probably established on the site of a much earlier illicit operation.

Just outside the town of Crieff, it was originally known as **Hosh** (Gaelic: *Cois*—"foot" of Glenturret), and it produces the malt whisky at the heart of the Famous Grouse Blend. Glenturret was one of the first distilleries to open a visitor center back in 1981, which was refurbished in 2002. Most distilleries today have associated visitor centers, but it isn't too far off the mark to say that with over one hundred twenty-five thousand visitors a year, Glenturret is more a visitor center with an associated distillery. In March of 2019 the ink dried on the Edrington Group's sale of the distillery to the Swiss based company Art & Terroir. Famous Grouse will remain in the group's hands.

About ten miles away is **Tullibardine** (Gaelic: *Tullach Bhardainn*—the "Hill of Warning"), set up in 1949 in the small village of Blackford. The water is drawn from the Danny Burn, which flows from the nearby Ochil Hills, tumbling over extinct volcanic rock and sandstones, which makes it extremely pure. Indeed, there is a tradition of great brewing in the area going back into the fifteenth century when its beers were enjoyed by kings. The burn is also the source for the Highland Spring bottled water company. In 1995, the then owners, Whyte & Mackay ceased production, but in 2003 it was resurrected by a private firm, that in turn sold it in 2011 to the French company, Picard Vins & Spiritueux.

The actual "Hill of Warning" is likely to be the rounded peak above the Tullibardine Wood, and the small farming community and chapel in the valley below. The origin of the name takes us back to a more violent time. There was nothing that the Lowlanders feared more than a Highland army, bekilted and charging forth from the mountains armed to the teeth. It scared the bejeesus out of them. The Romans recognized the threat and "closed" each of the glens leading out of the Highlands with forts, including Ardoch Camp which is very close by. It is not beyond the realms of fantasy to suggest that sentries were stationed on the hill (the Roman road runs behind Tullibardine Wood) to watch the entrances into the Highlands via Strathearn, Strathtay and the narrow Sma' Glen. The name might just be that old. Either way, Tullibardine's function as a lookout point and probable beacon lighting site is without question. It is not the only distillery whose name is rooted in a more warlike age.

The Highland Outliers

The politics and social history of the Scottish Highlands has always been complex and somewhat fraught. When we think of Highland history, we tend to envisage wild clansmen either raiding cattle or fighting never-ending feuds and vendettas. If by some miracle there is a consensus, then a common enemy would appear in the crosshairs: inevitably the Lowland Scots, the English, and fatally, the royal establishment during the Jacobite Civil Wars. Some of this is true of course, but it's something of a stereotype, indeed a cliché. Day-to-day living was hard, a subsistence way of life where bonds of family and clan could mean the difference between life and death. The chiefs had far higher ambition; and to many, their loyal clansmen were a means to an end.

The clan system (*clann*, from the Gaelic, meaning literally "children") evolved in the troubled days of the Wars of Independence (which ironically saw real power cemented in the Anglo-Norman south), and was a way by which ambitious young leaders and men with fire in their bellies could carve out some land by using the loyalty of those that followed them. After the collapse of the Lordship of the Isles in the fifteenth century, there was a domino effect across the mountains, where all sorts of robber barons saw opportunities to steal the scraps left by the dying entity—an entity that had once brought stability to the west. Other lordships would feel the aftershock; and the Highlands kind of developed a dual social hierarchy—loyalty and obedience to your chief by kin, and absolute loyalty to your feudal lord (who may be the same person).

From the fifteenth through the seventeenth centuries, the clans fought each other incessantly. Now, I don't want you to have Hollywood images of mass battles; most skirmishes involved less than a hundred men. But at times, and invoking in some cases their Norse heritage, they would bond in alliance and raid the rich Lowlands. This is why "Hills of Warning" were needed; but before they headed south, they had to come together—and deep in the mountains is Dalwhinnie.

In the very heart of the Highlands is an old lordship, Badenoch (Gaelic: *Bàideanach*—"drowned land"). This is an unforgiving country where several gateway valleys come together: Strathspey, Glen Spean, and Loch Ericht-side. Additionally, there are a number of strategic passes leading south such as the Gaick, Minigaig and most important of all, the Pass of Drumochter: the key link to Atholl and the Lowlands beyond.

At the northern end of Drumochter (Gaelic: *Druim Uachdar*—"ridge of the upper part") is a flat plain rising a little out from what would have been a landscape of bog and small lochs in days gone by (hence the "drowned land"). It sits at this important crossroads and was a key meeting point for clan forces converging from the west (various septs of Clan Donald, Macleod, MacLean, and Cameron), and from the far north (Frasers, MacKays, and Macintoshes, for example).

While waiting for the whole army to amass, and to prevent boredom, the chiefs and leaders developed games, trials, and competitions to keep their men busy. The type of events and trials undergone weren't random, of course— they prepared the clansmen for battle and could identify the top dogs. **Dalwhinnie** (Gaelic: *Dail Chunnaidh*—"Field of the Champion") takes us through the looking glass to this dramatic period of our history. These events would also be the origin of our modern Highland Games; the competitions at Dalwhinnie, however, must have been pretty tough affairs and quite bloody, no doubt.

A distillery was built there in 1897 by three partners who called it Speyside, but it went bust within the year. It was sold to AP Blyth, and in 1898, it was renamed Dalwhinnie. It is the highest distillery in Scotland, sitting at around eleven hundred feet above sea level, and seen from the modern A9 road with its classical pagoda roofing, it is exactly what you would expect a Highland distillery to look like. The name Speyside, however, lives on a little farther down the valley at Kingussie. **Speyside Distillery** (English—"On the River Spey") sits on the site of the old Tromie Mills, which ran from the early 1700s until 1965. Whisky production began in 1990 after a lot of effort and dedication by Mr. George Christie.

Further up the road, past the bleak Slochd Mór pass (Gaelic: *An Sloc*—"Great cleft"), is with sixteen stills one of the largest malt distilleries in Scotland: **Tomatin** (Gaelic: *Tom Aitionn*—"Hill of Juniper"). However, most of the outliers tend, like the Speyside Distillery, to be relatively small in scale; almost "craft production," and one of the best examples is **Royal Lochnagar** in Deeside (Gaelic: *Lochan na Gearr*—"The small lake of laughter"). Famed in song and story, the mountain Lochnagar (or more correctly *Beinn nan Ciochan*, the "Hill of Breasts"), is a beautiful peak crowning the Queen's Balmoral Estate in the heart of Royal Deeside.

The steep, snow-capped crags of the Black Spout dominate the landscape for travellers heading along the A93 from Aberdeen to Braemar, rising as it does out of a carpet of forest to the south.

The distillery itself lies at the foot of the mountain, about a half-mile or so from Balmoral Castle. The castle was acquired by Queen Victoria in 1848, and in the same year, she and Prince Albert visited the nearby distillery, which was founded in 1826 by the then owner John Begg. The couple was so impressed that they issued a warrant to allow the distillery to call itself Royal Lochnagar. Royal Brackla and the now defunct **Glenury Royal** (Gaelic: *Gleann Uaraidh*—"Glen of the Urie River") received their warrants from King William IV in the 1830s. (Laphroaig is currently by appointment to HRH Prince Charles, but doesn't use the term "Royal.")

Ben Nevis (Gaelic: *Beinn Neibhis*—the "Venomous Mountain") lies far to the west on the Atlantic coast by the town of Fort William (*An Gearasdan*—"the Garrison"), and is another distillery named for a famous mountain at the foot of which it sits. At 4,411 feet, Ben Nevis is Britain's highest peak and casts a long shadow over the region of Lochaber, a land where great mountains meet long fjords and deep glens. This was hardy country, home to numerous clans that had proved troublesome for far-off governments in Edinburgh and London—no more so than during the Jacobite Rebellions of 1689, 1715, and 1745.

In 1688 and 1689, during what is euphemistically called the "Glorious Revolution," King James VII and II, was removed from the throne in a bloodless coup, principally over the question of his religion. He was replaced by his son-in-law and nephew, William of Orange, and this action split Scotland in two. The charismatic John Graham of Claverhouse, Viscount Dundee, led a rebellion that, despite an initial success at the Battle of Killiecrankie collapsed at Dunkeld in August 1689. Another aborted attempt died on the frozen bogs of Sherrifmuir; and in 1745, Charles Edward Stuart got within a hundred miles of London with his Highland army before it too ended in catastrophe on the bloody field of Culloden in April 1746.

These rebellions against the establishment and the Crown drew their strength from a traditional source: Highland clansmen, loyal to the end. Lochaber was home to many of those clans that would gather at Dalwhinnie. The Camerons, the Macdonnells of Glengarry and Keppoch, MacDonald of Glencoe, and Stewart of Appin lay just across the water. Loch Linnhe, a long fjord, reaches deep into the hills there, and several key routes meet at the head of the loch, where the waters still achieve a reasonable depth. It was an ideal place for the government to build a fortress to keep watch on this threatening rebel country.

It's also a wet country, and fast flowing streams rush off the steep slopes of the Nevis Range toward the sea. As they reach the flat land around Fort William, they provide either the hydro power for the local aluminum smelter, or the water for the distillery, founded on the Allt a'Mhuilinn burn ("mill stream") in 1825. Since 1989 it has been in the ownership of the Japanese whisky firm, Nikka.

Farther down the coast is **Oban Distillery**, sitting slap-bang in the middle of a town that is younger than it is. This part of Argyll is known as Lorn, and Oban is a shortened version of the Gaelic *An t-Òban Latharnach*, which means the "Little Bay of Lorn." The distillery was founded in 1794, and the town that surrounds her is both charming and functional with great places to eat and drink and plenty to do. It is also the gateway to the Islands with several ferries plying daily to Mull, Lismore, and the Outer Hebrides.

In nearby Morven (*A' Mhorbairne*—the "Sea gap," which is well named given the geography at the mouth of Loch Linnhe) a new distillery began production in 2017: **Ncu'ean** (Gaelic: *Neachneohain*, probably—"Queen of Spirits").

The three remaining outliers all sit south of the Highland Line: **Deanston** (English—"Dean's Town") near the ancient strategic city of Stirling; **Glengoyne** (Gaelic: *Gleann Gainne*— named after Dumgoyne, which may mean "the point of the arrow," although "Glen of Wild Geese" or "Glen of Scarcity" have been suggested); and perhaps most interestingly linguistically, **Fettercairn** in Angus (Pictish/Gaelic: *Fothair Càrdain*—"Wooded Slope"). This makes a lot of sense—it is believed that the Pictish tribes in the Highlands protected the entrances to their key valleys with deep forests, the most famous being Birnam Wood. From the south, any invader would be faced with a line of hills and a thick barrier of trees (which they would assume ran deep into the mountains— but which didn't). Fettercairn lies right on the Highland Line close to one of the key passes into the lush valley of the Dee, so perhaps the name takes us back to these more warlike days. Alternatively, it could mean the sloped copse. Copses were woodlands used for periodic cutting, especially for tanning or charcoal production. Nearby is the old village of Kincardine, meaning "the head of the wood." My money's on the barrier.

The wide and diverse geography of the Highlands, from the Lennox around Loch Lomond to the flatlands of Caithness, has determined in many respects the distribution of distilleries, but it also highlights the various elements at work on its language heritage. As we have seen from this diverse set of whiskies, Gaelic is the predominant language. That is not a surprise, as this was the community language of the whole region (except northeast Aberdeenshire and Caithness) until the twentieth century, and Gaelic is at heart an agrarian language, one born of the land—as is whisky. But looking at the distribution—Brora in the north has a Norse influence, Deanston in the south is English, and Fettercairn in the east has Pictish remnants—it shows that the whiskies reflect the underlying dominance of fostered, borrowed, and archaic languages, and the subsequent enduring legacy this has left us with.

CHAPTER 9

CAMPBELTOWN

"Campbeltown Loch is a wonderful place, but the price of the whisky is grim; How good would it be, if the whisky was free, and the loch was filled up to the brim."

— "Campbeltown Loch, I Wish You Were Whisky"

Andy Stewart

Campbeltown is a bit of a geographical enigma, positioned as it is at the far end of Argyll's long Kintyre Peninsular (Gaelic: *Cinn Tire*—"Land's End"), about five miles from the Mull of Kintyre headland, made famous in song by Paul McCartney and a stone's throw away from Ireland.

Believe me, it's a long tedious drive to get to Campbeltown from anywhere. So, historically traveling by boat was realistically the only economical option; and the sea plays a huge part in the history of this part of Scotland. Much of the County of Argyll (Gaelic: *Earra-Ghàidheal*—"Coast of the Gael") is indented with fjords and surrounded by islands, such as Islay. It's the inheritor of a kingdom spanning Scotland and Ireland, and as such waterways have long been key to the region's prosperity. The sheltered waters of Campbeltown

Loch, one of the best natural harbors in Europe, sit at a vital crossroads, and so it emerged as a bustling place with strong trading links. In a way it can seem an island of sorts. But remoteness here is an illusion, one drawn from our modern reliance on the car. In the past, things were very different.

Then as now, overland travel down to the town was always somewhat arduous. So, unsurprisingly boat building became a mainstay industry. But, with clean water, a decent crop of barley from the fields around nearby Machrihanish (Gaelic: *Machaire Shanais*—"Plain of whispers"), and a benign climate gifted by the Gulf Stream, whisky making took off there as well. There was also a local source of coal from the seam at Drumlemble (Gaelic: *Druim Leamhan*—"Ridge of Elm trees"), which helped to heat the stills, amongst other things. A light rail system was built in 1773, which brought the coal into Campbeltown. An alignment of stars paved the way to the growth of the most spectacular whisky town the world has ever seen. And a similar adjustment would see it all come crumbling down.

Originally known as Ceann Loch Chille Chiarain (Gaelic: "the head of the loch of the church of Saint Ciarán"), the land was purchased in the second half of the seventeenth century by the Earl of Argyll, Archibald Campbell and renamed in his honor. A new town was built, and the population grew with the agricultural improvements, better sea-links to Ireland and connections up the Clyde to Glasgow and her ready market. Understandably, by the early nineteenth century, Campbeltown whisky was being readily sought after. By the end of the century, there were around thirty-four distilleries in operation, and the title of "Whisky Capital of the World" was well-deserved. As volumes increased, new markets in the United States opened up, and to a certain extent the producers started looking at quantity at the expense of quality. The seeds were being sown that would lead to the collapse of this most vibrant of regions.

Demand for malt whisky principally for blending meant that the quality had to be up to snuff, and too often for Campbeltown malts, this wasn't the case—so, they were overlooked by the big players. The taxes and economic strains brought about by the First World War, and suffered across the industry as a whole, widened the cracks, and the infrastructure was creaking. An increased reliance on the American market saw more and more eggs thrown into one basket, and when Prohibition was enacted, the wheels fell right off the trolley.

There was no one reason for the disintegration of the Campbeltown whisky industry; it was a buildup of incremental factors leading to the whole house of cards crashing down. The coal seam at Drumlemble was exhausted by 1923 and closed that year; the railway couldn't continue without that business, and it shut up shop in 1932; freight by boat was being replaced by road haulage, and that made the town remoter still; and Prohibition followed by the Depression sealed the deal. Eighteen distilleries closed in the 20s and 30s, leaving three: **Springbank** (English—"bank by the spring"), **Glen Scotia** (English/Gaelic—"valley of Scotland"), and **Meadowburn** (English—"meadow stream"). Meadowburn closed for good in 1986, and Springbank, today one of the most heralded whiskies in the industry, had long bouts of closure. Campbeltown was for a while in serious danger of losing all her production completely.

In 2000, **Glengyle** (Gaelic, probably—a shortening of Argyle, an older spelling of Argyll), which had been one of the casualties of the privations of the 1920s, was resurrected and started producing in 2004. The first whisky became available in 2014 and is known as **Kilkerran** (an English rendering of Chille Chiarain).

In a way, the story of Campbeltown is a reflection of the ups and downs in the story of Scotch as a whole; but the complete collapse of a place once called "Whiskyopolis" was spectacular for all that. Today, there are several expressions coming from Springbank, including another resurrected name, **Longrow** (English—"long row," a reference to ploughing), and both Glengyle and Glen Scotia show that the green shoots of recovery are returning to this hallowed home of whisky. The Scotch Whisky Association has once again recognized Campbeltown as a distinct and protected region. After a long hiatus, it all seems happily to be heading in the right direction.

PART 3

SLÀINTE MHATH

CHAPTER 10

WHISKY MAKING & DRINKING

"I never drink whisky without water,
and never drink water without whisky."

—Chic Murray

For newcomers to Scotch, it can all seem a little daunting— hard-to-pronounce names, cliquey terms, a seemingly unending set of rules, and a legion of specialists preaching their own whisky gospel, all leading you Pied Piper-like down the garden path to a cultish hell. There are clubs, academies, and associations; ambassadors and masters; writers and a raft of self-proclaimed experts out there; all of which makes it sound like some sort of secret society requiring rites of passage before you get into the "know." This snobbish view of whisky is old fashioned and unhealthy, but stubbornly hard to shift despite all the work being done by those who actually work in the industry.

Hopefully, this book will help peel away some of this, and show that Scotch is the drink of the people, not some kind of exclusive beverage reserved for the informed few. It is a part of the landscape and history of Scotland, and it's for everyone interested in trying and enjoying it. The making and drinking (the fun bit) of Scotch has a language and vocabulary all of its own. So, pour yourself another large one as we strip back the layers, expose the truth, and explode the myths of whisky making.

∽

There are two types of whisky made in Scotland: single malt and single grain; and married together, they create blended whisky (or if the malts alone are mixed, then a "vatted malt;" although, the term "blended malt" is, rather confusingly, also used). As we have seen, single grains like Cameronbridge or Invergordon use the continuous Coffey still and produce huge volumes of a light, high alcohol level spirit that can become vodka, gin, or whisky. By contrast, single malt distilleries use a batch system and employ pot stills and traditional manual methodology. Single grains can use a number of different ingredients, principally wheat, but also rye, maize, and some barley. Indeed, much of Scotland's wheat crop goes to the grain distilleries. Single malt whisky is exclusively 100 percent barley.

First cultivated in Mesopotamia's Fertile Crescent some 10,500 years ago, barley (*Hordeum Vulgare*) is the largest grain crop in Scotland with approximately 1.7 million tons harvested annually. It takes its name from the old English, *Bære*. Unsurprisingly, it is also the root of the word's beer and barn (literally, "barley house").

Today, few distilleries "malt" their barley in-house. But what does that mean? Here's one of those "in-the-know" terms, but it is surprisingly simple: traditionally, harvested barley was brought to the distillery by local farmers and it would then be laid out on stone floors to a depth of several inches and moistened in a warm environment. The idea was to trick the barley into thinking it was spring, and so it would begin to sprout. The Scotch industry uses what's called "two-row barley," as it has a higher fermentable sugar content than the alternative "six-row barley" (which is used in bourbon making, as they're only looking for the enzyme that turns starch to sugar, and not the volume). From the 1950s to the 1990s, the most common cultivar or strain used was Golden Promise, but that gave way to new varieties such as Optic. The distillers are looking for barley that has a high starch content, low nitrogen levels, and a short dormancy (the time between harvesting and the grain sprouting). The farmer obviously wants high yields so he can supply an ever-increasing demand, and his own profit margins. Therefore, there are always new strains coming online to continually advance this.

Figure 10.1 Peat cutting
(photo reproduced with permission of Tommy Tardie)

Just as the grain is about to germinate, the process is halted by warming the barley, which gives rise to some of the flavor profiles in the final product. The vast majority of the barley used in the Scotch industry today is dried using warm air at industrial maltings; but some, particularly those on Islay, Orkney or say Talisker on Skye, are dried by burning peat: however, not necessarily or exclusively on site.

Each year, organic material accumulates and rots in wet bogs across the Highlands and Islands. In this anaerobic environment, it can't fully decay, and the next year's layer is then added. Over thousands of years this forms a dark carbonizing material that is on the road to becoming coal. The peat bogs in parts of Scotland can be over thirty feet deep and began forming over four thousand years ago; and in all that time it has been the principal domestic fuel on the islands. The word peat first appeared in Scotland around 1200 within Latin texts, but is undoubtedly derived from an older Welsh source, meaning "piece," describing not the material, but its cutting into bricks.

The peat burns with an intense red heat and has a beautiful sweet aroma. Of course we're not trying to toast the barley, the heat is tempered in the kilns using water and it is the resultant smoke that actually dries the grain. Those smoke molecules coat each individual grain (with what distillers call phenols), and these elements are taken forward into the process. This is why some whiskies are smoky and others are not. It is a purely man-added influence and can thus be controlled—the longer the kilns burn, more phenols are added. Hence, some whiskies are smokier than others; it's all a matter of taste.

This germination and then drying process helps develop the enzymes that will turn the natural starches in the grain into sugar (mostly maltose sugar). This process is called "malting," and it's why we get malt whisky. It also breaks down the protein lattices that encage the starch, allowing the brewers to access the sugars. This is why other grain spirit producers include a small amount of barley in their production, as barley is the only commercial grain that can do this (although some today can use artificial enzymes).

The barley is then ground down in a mill and turned into grist (Old English, "to grind"), which is a mix of husk and flour (many distilleries employ a Porteous Roller Mill for the job). This is then placed into the mash tun, which is essentially a large cauldron where hot water is added in stages of temperature. The starch is converted into a sweet, sugary liquid called wort (from the Old English *wyrte*, meaning "new beer"). This is then piped into washbacks, where the yeast is added. The yeast then ferments the wort into wash, essentially a crude beer with an alcohol by volume of around 8 percent when the process is finished (the alcohol is a waste product from the yeast that eventually kills it). In some distilleries they call it "pundy," and in days gone by it was often quite an effort to keep the locals out of the distillery at night in case they syphoned off a bucket or two.

Figure 10.2 Glenfiddach washbacks
(photo reproduced with permission of Tommy Tardie)

Yeast, from the Old English, *gyst*, meaning "to boil or foam," is a unicellular fungus that is abundant in the wild where it thrives on decaying organic material such as fruit. It requires no energy from the sun to grow and reproduce, instead getting all the required nutrients from the natural sugars it feeds on. Observing nature, man inadvertently domesticated yeast thousands of years ago to make both bread and beer. In an aerobic (oxygen rich) environment, the yeast turns these sugars into carbon dioxide and water, but in an environment deprived of oxygen (anaerobic), it instead produces CO_2 and various alcohols. Bakers use the CO_2 to help the bread rise; brewers and distillers take advantage of the drinkable ethanol.

There remains the argument of beer before bread. Both are just about as difficult to make—but beer wins out slightly, and the traditional beers of Mesopotamia, for example, were probably just a bit more nutritious than the unleavened breads made in the region at the time. While today we know that yeast is the catalyst for turning organic material into alcohol, the process wasn't fully understood until the early twentieth century, and, indeed, we still don't completely understand why. Over the ages, following the same techniques repeatedly, the strains that would be good at making beer began to differ from those good at making wine, and so various varietals emerged. Modern brewers, vintners, and distillers cultivate the descendants of those archaic wild yeasts.

The yeast doesn't always just produce ethanol and will sometimes create other alcohols such as methanol. Also, there are other reactions bubbling away in the soup to produce organic compounds; things like fatty acids, esters, and aldehydes, all of which display different characteristics. These extras are known as "congeners" and are what gives the whisky much of its flavor (the term congener found common currency in the eighteenth century and comes from Latin, meaning "together with the stock").

Using different types of yeast will vary the recipe of these slightly. The yeasts most commonly used are all strains of the species *Saccharomyces Cerevisiue*, such as M, MX, Mauri, and Brewers & Distillers. Many of the distilleries will actually use a combination.

The wash, which is literally awash with alcohols and organic juices, is then sent through to the Still House, and this is where the real magic happens. In order to separate the alcohol from the water and to bring it up to a high enough proof, the wash is boiled twice in large copper kettles, or stills. Copper is the preferred metal, as it has a number of good qualities, such as removing sulphur, and it imparts no metallic flavor on the end product. It's also a malleable metal, which means it can be fashioned into almost any shape—and every distillery in Scotland has different shaped stills. This, in turn, affects the chemistry of the spirit, and thus the whisky. The pot still has two parts. The bottom bulbous part is known as the cucurbit (from Latin and essentially meaning "pumpkin shaped"); and the top or lid part, called the alembic, is a linquistic remnant of the Arabic word for the whole still: *al-anbīq*.

The internal temperature and pressure of the still, and the speed at which the liquid is boiled will all have an effect as well; it's quite the balancing act. The first distillation produces a liquid that is around 27 percent alcohol and known as "low wines." In days gone by when multiple distillations were required to bring up the proof, the next boiling produced "high wines." Today, after the second distillation, the end result is a clear spirit of around 70 percent alcohol by volume. The rest of the volume is made up of what are known as congeners, many of which are chemically transformed organic compounds with distinct flavors, longer-chain alcohols (some of which are desirable in small amounts), water, and a few other chemicals such as the phenols introduced from say the peat.

The word distill comes from the Latin, *distillare*, which translates as "trickle down in minute drops," which is a very good way to describe the process. The vapors of alcohol evaporate up the swan neck of the still, and along the lyne arm to the condenser, where it transforms back into a liquid. The length of the lyne arm and its angle also imparts certain properties upon the whisky. The term "lyne arm" is debatable. It could come from the Gaelic language for a pool, as certain angles could cause pooling; or more likely, from the early distillers, laying the tube down toward the condenser. In some distilleries, it's referred to as a "lyne pipe."

The clear liquid, the spirit (the term spirit comes from alchemy in the fourteenth century and means "volatile substance"), then flows through the 'spirit safe' into a collecting tank.

This safe is a large glass box framed in brass and was invented in the 1820s when new tax regulations were introduced. At this point in the process, the spirit is now liable for taxation, but in reality this duty isn't paid until the whisky leaves the warehouse after maturation. Until 1983, there were resident taxmen at each distillery, and only they and the manager together could open the safe—in order to prevent anyone from stealing un-taxed spirit. However, the stillman needs access to the liquid as it runs through in order to separate the drinkable ethanol from the poisonous methanol and other undesirable compounds (fusel alcohols, for example). As such, the safe is fitted with external taps that remotely work hydrometers, valves, and other instruments that determine the specific gravity of the alcohol. When it changes, they can turn handles to redirect the liquid into different tanks. It is ingenious, and the safes are usually beautifully crafted brass cabinets that form the focal point of the still house.

Figure 10.3 Macallan stills
(photo reproduced with permission of Tom Hughes)

From there, the spirit is piped over to the warehouse where it is then put into oak casks for maturation. Oak is the only wood that can be used, as it allows the whisky to breathe and evaporate off the more volatile and radical molecules, thus smoothing it out. And it does so uniqulely among wood without the spirit leaking. The choice of high-quality casks is crucial in the process and having a good wood management policy is vital to long-term and viable success.

The barrels used in maturing Scotch are, barring a couple of experimental examples, second hand. That is, they've previously held something else. In America, the bourbon industry by law must only use brand new American oak barrels, so there is a constant turnover and supply of used casks with an eager market overseas. Consequently, the vast majority of Scotch is matured in ex-bourbon barrels.

The first time that newly made Scotch spirit is put into the cask is known as "first fill," then when it gets re-used again, "second fill," and so on. Older, spent casks are often used for mixing the whiskies together prior to bottling in a process called "marrying." In old age they become garden center plant pots. For malts that will have an age-statement of say twelve years, they will be poured from scores of casks of varying ages—but none younger than twelve years by law—into large vats, married and piped to the bottling plant.

Other barrel types often used include ex-sherry, ex-port, and ex-wine; and each imparts different and unique characteristics onto the whisky. It is common practice to use a mix of both bourbon and sherry casks, or to "finish" a whisky in a second barrel type. This leads to labels on the bottles such as double wood, or sherry finish, and so on. As consumers have become more sophisticated and knowledgeable about whisky, the labels have become more informative, including more information on the barrel provenance, flavor profiles, and alcohol by volume signatures. Today, there is less and less emphasis on age statements. The reasons for doing this are partially a desire to create great whisky, and partly to manage barrel stock.

At this point, the single malt is going to head in one of two directions: to the bottling plant, or to the blending plant (and terminally the same bottling plant).

The blending labs of most companies are the heart and soul of the final expressions that we enjoy off the shelf; where the mastery of the distiller and timely knowledge of the warehouse manager are crafted to the original vision.

Then come the suits sitting around IKEA tables who further entrust the boots on the ground to get liquid to lips. Even single malts are fashioned in these labs, where the correct balance of cask types, ages, and so on is brought together, and the blenders choose the right recipe: it's like baking a cake.

For blended Scotch this is even more complex, and much of the decision rests on the collective expertise and noses of the lab team, and in particular the master blender. Whisky is inconsistent, as you'd expect, with each barrel bringing something slightly different to the party. The job of selecting the right cask, at the right age, and with the right volume percentage, is one of the most amazing parts of the whole story. I've met a few master blenders in my time, and my hat comes off each and every time to what they achieve.

You will often see the statement on the bottle "Single Cask," usually accompanied with a bottle numbering. These are hand-selected individual barrels that are bottled as a batch, and the choice is usually a collaboration between the blender, boardroom, and distillery manager. This is also the realm of the private bottler, and this is when it can be a bit complicated. Private bottlers, such as Gordon & Macphail or Signatory, buy casks from the bigger companies, hand-picked in advance, and aged according to their specifications. This means you can find bottles of say, Glenlivet, out there that are not bottled and sold by Pernod or Macallan's with different barrel types and ages than the usual distillery releases. Independents also tend to play around with the alcohol levels (the mainstream companies will do this as well, especially when releasing limited editions or looking for publicity) often selling their wares at what is known as "cask strength whisky," which can range in alcohol by volume percentages from the high 40s to the low 60s.

At the bottling stage, water is added to reduce the ABV down to 40 percent for blends and 43 percent for malts (this will vary from market to market; and some expressions, such as Talisker, prefer a higher level). So, if you hear people say that they don't put water in their whisky, you can remind them that it has already been done for them. You may also hear people talk about the "proof," especially in the United States, where it is commonly found on bourbon labels.

In days gone by, on ships crossing the Atlantic from Britain to America, sailors were entitled to a shot of rum in the morning and another in the evening; all part of King's Regulations. This rum however would be "watered" down using lime juice (it's why Americans call Britons "limeys") to help prevent scurvy. Some unscrupulous captains would water the rum right down, as they didn't want their men bouncing off the rigging; but by regulation the sailors had the right to demand from the captain or the bursar that he prove that the alcohol level was correct. The only ABV that can be proved at sea is 57.15 percent, which is derieved at by soaking the rum in gunpowder and then igniting it. It will only burst into flames when the alcohol levels are 57.15 percent and higher. So, that level (rounded to 57 percent) became known as "navy strength rum," and declared to be 100 degrees of proof, a calculation of around x1.75.

Technically the ABV in the UK, going back to the 1500s was calculated by multiplying the proof by the fraction $\frac{4}{7}$. Thus a single malt with an ABV of 43 percent will have a proof value of 75.25 degrees. In 1816, the calculation using gunpowder was replaced with the more accurate 'specific gravity.' In the States, the proof is calculated by solution in water two to one, hence: 50 percent ABV = 100 degrees of proof. Producers haven't put a proof statement on a bottle of alcohol in the UK since the early 1980s, and even in the States, it's done more for tradition than by law.

The "Angels' Share" is the rather quaint term given to the annual evaporation of alcohol from the casks into the atmosphere, without which maturation could not take place. Greater at the start, as more volatile and energetic molecules are released (those pesky hangover-inducing fusels), and slowing down as the whisky gets older, the average in Scotland is around a 2 percent volume loss per year out of the cask. Ever visit a distillery, and you'll see the trees and walls around the warehouses are all black; this is actually an alcohol loving fungus (*Baudoinia Compniacensis*), and is a sure indicator of airborne ethanol. As well as having internal effects on the nature of the maturing whisky, this annual loss also means a continual diminution of volume, and thus return on investment. It is therefore fundamentally linked to shelf-price.

Figure 10.4 Balvenie casks
(photo reproduced with permission of Tommy Tardie)

But that's only part of the story. Very old whiskies command high prices, partly because the juice had to spend so long in the cask, and partly due to a dearth of potential buyers for the subsequent rarity (*really* limited editions). That said, the whisky itself may not be that great—so much time in the barrel will see a lot of wood influence, perhaps too much, and wood choices fifty or sixty years ago was not as quality-controlled as it is today. There's also provenance—these limited, aged whiskies may have significant meaning; perhaps bottled for a special occasion, or in conjunction with other high-end products.

A fine example would be the Bowmore that was "casked" by the Queen on her visit in 1977, and then bottled by her in 1992. This Royal collection has been auctioned off to raise money for the many charities that the Queen is head of, and as gifts for important foreign presidents and prime ministers—a wheel-greasing ploy, and an effective one. The occasional "Whisky Galore" bottles that still wash ashore from the wreck of the SS *Politician* (which was carrying twenty-eight thousand cases of Scotch when it sank off the coast of the Western Isles in 1941) are the stories of legend on the Islands and far beyond, spawning a bestseller and two movies. And these bottles can now reach astronomical value—way beyond the value of the juice itself.

Price, however, even at a more modest level, is still a good indicator of quality and value; more so than a simple age statement. People often confuse age with maturity, and it is the latter that is much more important, and key to the whisky's success. Distillery managers and the team of blenders leave little to chance. The whiskies you see on the shelf are not lucky-breaks but designed to have certain qualities and profiles appealing to a broad church of consumers. This means a true marriage of all the elements from still shapes, wood management, and of course, the length of time the spirit needs to mature to reach the sought-after finished product. The bean counters also have a say, so that the company will profit on what it makes; and it is a combination of these and other more ethereal factors that determine: a) the price of the whisky in the store, and b) the age statement, if any. As most single malts are in fact drawn from numerous casks of roughly the same age, there will still be discrepancy. A twelve-year-old, for example, cannot have whisky in that bottle under that age, but it could conceivably have fourteen or fifteen year olds in there to maintain consistency. Blended whiskies go through the same rigor, but are mixes from different distilleries.

So, a ten-year-old from one distillery may be at the same level of maturity as a fourteen-year-old from another—it is simply a combination of desired maturation for the spirit character, volumes available, costs incurred, and appeal of a particular price point at market for the quality and popularity of the brand. Levels of stock are also critical. Much of what's on the market now was laid down when whisky was just coming out of the doldrums and production levels were comparatively low; that means shortages—essentially, demand outstripping supply. So, most producers play around with different barrel finishes (this lengthens the life of the hard-working bourbon barrel) and non-age statements, which gives them freedom to play around with younger whisky. Younger whisky also has a different set of characteristics than older ones (less wood influence and more fermentation/distillation influence), and for consumers keen to try anything new, they've come into their own to a certain extent. This trend, believe me, is just in its infancy.

There are still the old-fashioned sticklers out there who won't buy less than fifteen- or twenty-one-year-olds or whatever; it's all part of the snobbery. But if they're willing to spend hundreds of pounds on whisky that may taste just as good as one that costs £50, then let them—it all helps the guys back home.

Price by contrast doesn't tend to mislead as much, and by and large you get what you pay for in quality, up to around the £500 mark, beyond which you're buying the label as much as the liquid. If you investigate, it becomes apparent that there seems to be step-ups in prices, from say (and this is supermarket manipulation aside) £30 to £40 per

185

bottle to £60 to £80 and so on; and this gives you a good indication that you are also stepping up in terms of quality, smoothness, and maturity. At the end of the day, you are the consumer—but be educated, tailor your taste to your wallet, and you won't be disappointed. Above all, do not listen to the self-appointed experts. You are the expert when it comes to what you like and don't like to eat or drink. So, to that end, and indeed to wrap this story up, go on—grab one final dram tonight and join us for a wee session.

Figure 10.5 Nosing at Blair Athol
(photo reproduced with permission of Visit Scotland)

EXIT THROUGH THE SHOP:
THE ART OF DRINKING WHISKY

So, the bottle is bought, the ambience is right, and it's time to open and enjoy the dram. To me, whisky isn't an ornament; it ought to be drunk, and gathering dust is a heinous crime. But again sadly there are too many out there who have added far too much complexity into what is, after all, a personal enjoyment of a great drink. You don't need to be inundated with an array of nose and flavor profiles, or people telling you it smells like lavender on a winter morning, or like Labrador puppies, or whatever. These never-ending tasting notes are simply people's opinions (I trust those of the distillers and blenders, however, as they really are experts), and are no better or attuned than yours—it's their vocabulary that has been honed. Your nose and tongue are unique, and if what you get doesn't match some sort of checklist, throw away the checklist and make your own. We all share a very basic set of taste senses and over four hundred nasal senses—of which, no two human beings (even identical twins) share more than two hundred. I simply do not smell and register the world, or indeed the whisky in my hand, as you do. So, are you still relying on a guy's tasting notes in some book? Do not be intimidated—it's a brave new world, and it's yours!

I'm not a fan of telling people how to drink or enjoy their whisky, but throughout my career I've met some incredible people who have taught me how best to enjoy my dram—and without an ounce of pretentiousness. So, in the same vein:

Pour yourself a decent dram, go on…a *decent* dram—this is educational after all. If you want to pour it over ice, go ahead—there are no rules, remember. Personally, I'd suggest playing around with different styles and ways to drink your whisky first, until you find the style that suits your palate and sense of enjoyment. At the end of the day, if you like it, drink it. So, let's assume a neat pour to start with—it's time to enliven the senses.

First of all, have a look at the whisky; hold the glass up and give it a swirl and see the viscosity, the surface tensions, and the wonderful color, from barley gold to rich mahogany. As it settles, you will see lines of liquid slowly return; these are known as legs. You may hear a great deal about the legs and what you can divine from them. In short, however, the characteristics of these runs, be they languid or watery, wide or thin, can come from a myriad of potential sources in the production, and so to be honest they're not really worth bothering about. There may well be bubbles on the surface of the whisky, first noticeable when you originally poured your glass. These are known as pearls, and from these you can tell if the whisky is mature or young, high or low proof (high proof or older whiskies produce bigger or a greater amount of bubbles that tend to last longer). So, if a whisky has no age statement but you know the ABV (it'll be on the bottle), then you can deduce something of the maturity of your dram. Fun stuff.

Food experts tell us that we will enjoy a meal or a drink more once we have a look at it; it draws on memories of past pleasant experiences, and the brain sends signals that release hormones that will actually enhance how we taste it. A picture of a juicy steak on television gets me slavering, and that's just a visual. Once your nose gets in on the act, the body ups the ante.

Your sense of smell is unique; it is the only key sense that is hotwired directly into your brain—all the others have to go through the clearing station in your hypothalamus, which is an ancient appendage to your brain going back to the days when we were fishes. Its job is to filter out all the irrelevant stuff like the taste of the roof of your mouth preventing cerebral overload. By contrast, everything you smell (consciously or otherwise) is funneled through the olfactory bulb, which is an annex of the brain and allows you to distinguish thousands of different odors. This was important from an evolutionary point of view, but as the location in the brain, where much of this is processed, is so close to our long-term memory center, smell is so much associated with our past and emotion. Thus, what we smell in our drink is fundamental to how we will appreciate it.

The trick here is to be fully committed. Stick your nose right into the glass and sniff two or three several deep nasal breaths, so that you really feel it. The ethanol hitting your olfactory bulb will make your eyes water, so give yourself a minute, and do it again. This time you'll find that your nose recovers more quickly; it's becoming acclimatized. Then, start to smell the whisky—get your nose right into the glass and breathe normally. Now, you only ever breathe out of one nostril at a time, and it switches every seven minutes, so waft the glass back and forth. Now that you've overcome the sharp alcohol tingle, you will start to take in some of the aromas, which unbeknown to you are getting your gastric juices flowing. You don't need to put what you smell into words, but if things jump out, write them down. Think more about whether it's sweet, smoky, or fruity, and that kind of thing. Once you start talking about apple cider on the Fourth of July, you're on a slippery slope.

Repeat the nosing as long as you want, and if you need to cleanse the senses, take a couple of sniffs of cold water. But eventually, the time comes to drink. I always advise to take a tiny sip and drink it right down as quickly as possible—not trying to taste. After a few seconds, you'll feel a warm glow in your solar plexus; this is your body reacting to the ethanol. Thankfully, your body is geared up to accepting alcohol, and there are ten enzymes in your liver whose sole function is to turn ethanol into energy. Indeed, if you decided to go "on the wagon" (a term that dates from Prohibition, when those driving the trucks or wagons of booze weren't allowed to drink on the job) for good, despite your puritanical smugness, your body will start to produce ethanol artificially regardless. Don't fight it.

Once the glow has dissipated, take another sip, and this time roll it around your mouth, letting it coat your palate and tongue; then swallow. There will be less burn (Scotches tend to burn or tingle at the front of your mouth, your lips, and so on, while bourbons tend to rasp the throat—just the nature of the grains and the methodology of distillations), and you will pick up more nuances this time. Again, let's not think about flavors as such, but mouthfeel. Where do you feel the sensation? Is it viscous and rich, or is it light and watery? Is there an initial *whoomph* and gone, or is there a lingering set of flavors, known as a finish? These are all considerations before we even think about how it tastes. If this seems somewhat convoluted, don't panic. Most, if not all, of this is instinctive; this is just about talking though a process.

In all of this, it is hard to avoid actually tasting anything and zoning it out, simply because taste is also there to stop you from eating stuff that is bad for you. Now, if the whisky tingles and bites at the tip and sides of your tongue, then you can infer that it matured in a barrel made of American white oak (*Quercus Alba*), but if the weight and sensation is initially at the back of the mouth, then you can say with some certainty that the barrels were made of European oak (*Quercus Robar*); and this is a great piece of information to impress people at parties.

Napoleon believed that to rule the world you needed ships, and to have a great fleet (in order to defeat the Royal Navy) you needed plenty of oak trees. Looking at the great forests of Northern Spain or Southern France, he harvested plenty, but he had a sustainable policy of replanting, which has meant that many of these great woods have survived, regenerated, and thrived in the two hundred years since. Many sherry makers use casks made from trees cut from the forests of Galicia, Cantabria, and Asturias, while cognac producers tend to use wood from Troncai in France. Scotch producers who rely on sherry casks work very closely with their colleagues in Spain to ensure availability. The Spanish forests are thus deliberately managed (with an annual incremental wood growth in excess of seventeen million cubic feet).

These great forests look on with fortitude to the wide and stormy Bay of Biscay, where hoary winds rattle off the Atlantic and drive through the hulks. As such, the trees are broad-trunked and slow growing. This makes them tannin rich, and the drying or toasting processes before their usage in the sherry industry does not remove them fully. Tannin is bitter, and this is why you pick it up at the back of the tongue. American white oak, which also grows in sustainable forests in the Midwest, has a shorter growing season, and thus stretches for the skies when summer suns are bright. This makes the tree rich in vanillin, which as the name suggests is similar to vanilla. The charring process in the bourbon industry essentially caramelizes these sugars, producing that rich toffee flavor you associate with bourbon. This is, of course, sweet; thus, you get the tingle at the front of the mouth.

The industry does like to mix it up a bit—some sherry casks are matured in American oak, and by adding new tops and bottoms, spiciness is developed. By this point, don't even try to wrap your tongue or brain around it—just stick the slippers on the coffee table, put on Netflix, and enjoy the juice. But before we wrap this up, there is one last myth that needs to be laid to rest. The Holy Grail of whisky lore that seems to be unyielding: water!

The pithy quote at the start of this chapter from Chic Murray is a classic from a great Scottish comedian, a man whose droll, deadpan humor could make the mundane and everyday funny. His one-liners are legendary and comical because we can all relate to them. Adding water to whisky is seen by many to be a sin. Chic Murray in this one line—"I never drink whisky without water, and I never drink water without whisky"—not only alludes to chronic alcoholism, but pokes fun at the so-called aficionados and their never-ending set of rules when it comes to whisky. And in doing so, makes it nonsense. I was once told by a blender that if anyone ever said that I shouldn't put water in my whisky, then they didn't understand the science of flavor. So, let's do some debunking.

As we've seen, water is important at several stages of the process: malting, mashing, condensing the spirit, and at bottling, but adding water to your whisky in your glass, hands you the power to alter the flavors and characters for good or ill. Water doesn't necessarily make a whisky worse or better, but it does alter how you taste it. Again, much of the why belongs in the realm of the organic chemist, but there are certain key elements that anyone with a tongue can garner.

Alcohol is an anesthesia; it literally numbs your mouth, and the higher the ABV, the more so this is true. This inhibits the types and range of flavors that your tastebuds can distinguish. Normally, your tongue can pick out sweet, salt, bitter, sour, and a meaty feel called umami (we don't need to concern ourselves with this, as it isn't present in whisky); and a rainbow of identifiable tastes in between such as fruity, citrus, smoky, grassy, and so on. But as you climb into the world of the cask-strength whiskies, this ability is diminished. It may also seem fiery due to a chemical produced during distillation, which carries many of the same signatures as capsicum, the molecule that gives chili peppers their heat.

Water added at bottling, reducing the ABV usually to 43 percent, brings the whisky flavor into the tolerable range for most drinkers, and even neat, some people will enjoy the intensity of the sensation and mouthfeel in tandem with the flavors your tongue can pick up with alcohol at this strength. In order to be able to taste anything at all, your mouth produces saliva; this interacts with whatever food or drink has been ingested and allows the sensors on the tastebuds to do their job. Saliva is naturally slightly alkaline; whisky on the other hand is naturally acidic. The combination of the two helps in bringing to life the flavors.

Now, add some water—just a few drops to start with. You can really play around with this until you get a combination right for you. Have a look into the glass as you pour in the water—you'll see swirling, known as viscimetric whorls, and they occur when two liquids of different density meet (you will hear characters talk about the oils breaking—tune them out). This actually raises the temperature of the whisky by a couple of degrees, which in turn releases more molecules into the atmosphere, so repeat some of the nosing techniques as before. If the smell seems richer, then you're on the right path; if the smell seems somewhat muted, then not so. Not all whiskies were born to have water added. The fun is in the exploring.

Now, when you taste the whisky again, the burning sensation at the front of the mouth and on the tip of the tongue should be somewhat reduced, now that the alcohol levels are lower; this makes the whisky straight away feel cooler, and for some people, more manageable. Roll the whisky around the tongue, and hopefully you immediately pick out a greater depth of flavor profiles, and across different parts of the mouth. For some people, adding water moderates the sensation; the weight and mouthfeel, and these "new" flavors, appear more languid (literally watered down), and the trade off is not a good exchange. This is why some do not like to add water to their whisky and can be quite evangelical about it. What they fail to realize is that it all boils down to the preference of the individual.

Adding water doesn't change the flavor of the whisky as such; it allows the tongue to pick up characteristics and nuances it couldn't due to the higher alcohol strength. You may start to pick up say, greater fruitiness, malty notes possibly (like a hay barn), butteriness, and this kind of thing. Where your whisky had an intense smoky nature, now perhaps there is some salt there. Much depends on the chemistry that went before, and the barrels used in the maturation, but with a few drops of water hopefully you will experience a different (not necessarily better—you may prefer the smoke to the salt) set of sensations.

Now, good whisky should be drunk in good company, preferably around a peat fire, and in coming together in an act of communion you draw back to the oldest roots of whisky's story—a drink for the common man, for engaging friends, and telling of tales and stories. And with each pour, we honor this heritage and the company we keep with the age-old toast, "*slàinte mhath*," from the Gaelic, meaning literally "good health." *CLINK*. Go on have another—you know you want to!

ABOUT THE AUTHOR

David **McNicoll** was born and raised in the Scottish Highlands, and after leaving Aberdeen University where he gained an honors degree in geography, he went to work at a local distillery, Blair Athol. From there, he moved to the Scottish capital, Edinburgh, where he started working with a travel company specializing in small group tours of Scotland, and in 2004, he set up his own firm called Scottish Routes, which was dedicated to whisky and ancestral travel. David moved to America in 2010 and has represented several Scotch whiskies as Brand Ambassador in New York. Most recently, he is looking after Kilchoman and Penderyn single malts amongst others, adding another feather to his cap in terms of understanding the world of spirits. In addition, he hosts night classes in the history of Scotland and freelances as a whisky specialist in private tasting sessions across the city.

David retains close connections with friends and family back in Scotland, returning when he can—especially in the capacity as a member of the last private regiment in Europe, the Atholl Highlanders: a ceremonial guard raised by the Duke of Atholl. He is married to an American lass and has six-year-old twins to keep him on his toes.

CPSIA information can be obtained
at www.ICGtesting.com
Printed in the USA
BVHW042339050721
611171BV00012B/1812

9 781733 568210